Healthy Exchanges® Cookbook

ALSO BY JOANNA M. LUND

The Best of Healthy Exchanges® Food Newsletter '92 Cookbook

Notes of Encouragement

The Health Wagon Journal™

It's Not a Diet, It's a Way of Life® (audiotape)

It's Not a Diet, It's a Way of Life®

Healthy

Exchanges®

Cookbook

JoAnna M. Lund

G. P. Putnam's Sons / New York

G. P. Putnam's Sons
Publishers Since 1838
200 Madison Avenue
New York, NY 10016

Library of Congress Cataloging-in-Publication Data

Lund, JoAnna M.
    Healthy Exchanges® cookbook / by JoAnna M. Lund.
        p.   cm.
    Includes index.
    ISBN 0-399-14065-4
    1. Quick and easy cookery.   2. Reducing diets—Recipes.   3. Low-
fat diet—Recipes.   4. Low-cholesterol diet—Recipes.   I. Healthy
Exchanges, Inc.   II. Title.
    TX833.5.L86   1995   94-42173 CIP
    641.5'63—dc20

Before using these or any other collection of nutritional recipes, consult
your physician or health provider to be sure they are appropriate for you.
The information in this book is not intended to take the place of any
medical advice. It reflects the author's experiences, studies, research, and
opinions regarding healthy eating. All material included in this publication
is believed to be accurate. The publisher assumes no responsibility for any
health, welfare, or subsequent damage that might be incurred from use of
these materials.

Book design by Richard Oriolo

Printed in the United States of America

30 29 28 27 26 25 24

For more information about Healthy Exchanges® products, contact:
Healthy Exchanges, Inc.
PO Box 124
DeWitt, Iowa 52742-0124
(319) 659-8234

This book is printed on acid-free paper. ♾

This cookbook is dedicated in loving memory to my parents, Jerome and Agnes McAndrews, who bestowed on me their earthly talents. I am indebted to my mother for the artistic approach I take in creating recipes and to my father for the analytical skills involved in making the exchanges come out right even when using the whole can!

I want to share the last poem my mother wrote just hours before she joined my father in Heaven. I often wonder if she knew how comforting the last written words would be to her family. I hope this poem comforts you as well.

I Know

I know there is a God, because
I feel His presence everywhere.
I know there is a God, for
He has taken me in His care.

Sometimes I doubt Him,
When I think my prayers go unheard,
Yet, I know He is aware of what
I am praying for, every single word.

He answers in His own way
According to His will.
So, I place my worries in His hands
And tell my heart . . . be still.

—AGNES CARRINGTON McANDREWS

Acknowledgments

I'm just a common person with a very common problem, and I solved it with common sense. The rest of the story couldn't have happened without all the people who believed in my common sense and helped me realize my dream of sharing "common folk" recipes with the rest of the world. For dreaming with me, I want to express my thanks:

To Cliff Lund, my truck-drivin' man, who quit trucking to truck me around. It takes a strong guy to leave his "macho" profession as a long-haul trucker to work full-time with his wife in her business, and then have it be *healthy* recipes.

To John Duff, my editor, who saw my vision when I explained my "living and cooking in the real world" concept and helped me focus my goals.

To Barbara Alpert, who learned early on that I can't spell and that my new ideas had to be captured on paper almost as fast as she could finish the last batch. She helps me do the best I can . . . *the best I can.*

To Angela Miller and Coleen O'Shea, who took this small-town, middle-aged woman "as-is" and never considered turning me into "big-city."

To Greg Buttle and Bob Rowley, for saying "We've got to meet that woman from Iowa!" and then helping me plan a healthy recipe for proper business growth.

To David and Nancy Ramacitti, for helping me verbalize my dreams and saying "Gee whiz, why not?"

To Rose Hoenig, R.D., for computing the diabetic exchanges and answering my "common folk" nutritional questions in "common folk" medical language.

To Shirley Morrow, for typing my recipes ever since the very first recipe (Mexicalli Pie) was scribbled down on my trusty legal pad.

To my Healthy Exchanges® Helpers, who give me their all so I can give my all to recipe creation . . . Pam, Loretta, Gayle, Mary, Sandy, Meg, Jean, Ruth, Betty, Phyllis, Judy, Dot, Kris, Beth, and Lori.

To Tom, Judy, Mary Ann, and Brian at the Copy Shop. I never would have started the newsletter or written three cookbooks in less than three years' time without the Copy Shop Gang's encouragement.

To my sisters, Mary Benischek and Regina Reyes, and their children, for being my staunch cheerleaders all the way.

To my children, Tom Dierickx, James and Pam Dierickx, and Becky and John Taylor, for saying "That a way, Mom!"

And to my newest taste testers, Zachary and Joshua Dierickx. Those two beautiful boys can put a smile on Grandma's face just by being in the kitchen with me.

Last, but not least, to God, for giving me the talent to create "common folk" recipes in the first place. I will take credit for the chopping of the onions and even for the washing of the dishes, but not for the ideas that flow like water.

Foreword

I have been delighted and inspired in my work with JoAnna Lund and Healthy Exchanges®. It is wonderful to have such a tried-and-true resource for my patients who are working to manage diabetes and heart disease or simply trying to change to a healthy diet. They can be confident that these recipes are acceptable and workable in their meal plans and always high in flavor. The best part, of course, is that they are such "normal" foods that anyone would want to eat them.

You can easily use these recipes as part of a total healthy diet with the addition of fruits, vegetables, milk, starches, and lean proteins as needed. Eating for good health doesn't have to be the same old "diet foods." Any of these recipes will easily fit into your recommended meal plan.

"Pie in the sky!" Well, it seems that cooking the low-fat, low-sugar way has reached new limits, and we can all thank Healthy Exchanges® for giving many of us a helping hand.

Rose Hoenig, RD

Contents

How It All Began:
JoAnna Lund and the
Creation of Healthy
Exchanges®

For twenty-eight years I was the diet queen of DeWitt, Iowa. I tried every diet known—at least every one I could afford and was available to me in a small town in eastern Iowa. Any new method that promised to "melt away the pounds" tempted me to deprive my body in yet another way. I gobbled diet candies, took thyroid pills, fiber pills, prescription and over-the-counter diet pills. I even sent away for expensive "miracle" diet pills. I starved myself on the Cambridge Diet and the Bahama Diet. I went to endless weight-loss group meetings and sabotaged programs such as Overeaters Anonymous, Weight Watchers, and TOPS. I ate strange concoctions and rubbed on even stranger potions. I tried liquid diets. I attended individual and group hypnotism classes. I tried reflexology and even had an acupuncture device stuck in my ear!

Does this sound familiar? No wonder weight loss is a billion-dollar industry!

Each program I tried seemed to work at first. Losing that first five or ten pounds would get me so excited—and persuade me that this, at long last, would get the weight off. But inevitably, after the initial excitement wore off and the diet's routine and boredom set in, I'd quit. The pills were shoved to the back of the medicine chest, the cans of powder pushed to the rear of the kitchen cabinets, the program materials filed at the bottom of the closet; and once more, I felt like a failure.

In most cases, I'd quickly gain back the weight I'd lost, along with a few extra "souvenir" pounds that seemed always to settle around my hips and carry on a convention.

Like so many people, I've done the diet-lose-weight-gain-it-all-back "yo-yo" on the average of once a year. Over the years I've easily lost 1,000 pounds—and gained back 1,150 pounds.

When I was twenty years old, my weight was in the normal range for my height and build, although like many young women, I didn't think so. I was convinced I was fat and unattractive. At twenty-one, I was almost thin. (I have the photos to prove it!) At twenty-five, I might have been described as pleasingly plump. At thirty I was just plain overweight. At thirty-five I was almost thin, again. By forty I was once more pleasingly plump. At forty-five I'd become downright obese.

JoAnna at 300 pounds in 1990   *JoAnna today, a healthy size 14*

Now I'm fifty—and I'm 130 pounds less than my all-time high of around 300 pounds. I've kept the weight off for nearly three years now. I'd like to lose another ten pounds, but I'm not obsessed about it. If it takes me two or three years to accomplish it, that's okay.

What changed to help me jump off the roller coaster I was on? For one thing, I no longer looked to food to solve my emotional problems. But what really shook me up—and got me started on a new road—was Operation Desert Storm in early 1991. I sent three children off to the Persian Gulf war—my son-in-law, Matt, a medic in Special Forces; my daughter, Becky, a full-time college student and member of a medical unit in the Army Reserve; and my son James, a member of the Inactive Army Reserve who was reactivated as a chemicals expert.

Somehow, knowing that my children were putting their lives on the line got me thinking about my own mortality—and I convinced myself that the last thing they needed while they were overseas was to get a letter from home saying that their mother was ill because of a food-related problem.

The day I drove the third child to the airport to leave for Saudi Arabia, something happened to me that would change my life for the better—and forever. I stopped praying my perpetual prayer as a professional dieter, which was simply "Please, God, let me lose ten pounds by Friday." Instead, I prayed, "God, please help me not to be a burden to my kids and my family." I quit praying for what I wanted and started praying for what I needed—and in the process my prayers were answered. I couldn't keep the kids safe— that was out of my hands—but I could try to get healthier to better handle the stress of it. It was the least I could do on the home front.

Does that sound dramatic? Well, for me it was. It was the beginning of the new JoAnna Lund. My initial goal was not to lose weight or create recipes. I wanted to become healthier so I would be better able to handle this extraordinarily stressful time.

Each of my children returned safely from the Persian Gulf war. But something didn't come back—the 130 extra pounds I'd been lugging around for far too long. I'd finally accepted the truth after all those agonizing years of suffering through on-again, off-again dieting. There are no "magic" cures in life. No "magic" potion, pill, or diet will make unwanted pounds disappear.

I found something better than magic, if you can believe it. I discovered a new way to live my life—and uncovered an unexpected talent for creating "common folk" healthy and easy-to-prepare recipes. And I learned that I could motivate others to change their lives and adopt a positive outlook. I like to say *"When life handed me a lemon, not only did I make healthy, tasty lemonade. I wrote the recipe down!"*™

What I finally found—the "answer"—was not a quick fix or a short-term diet, but a great way to live well for a lifetime.

I want to share it with you.

An Introduction to
Healthy Exchanges®

Y ou want to eat healthy. Or maybe you need to lose a few pounds—or a few more than that. But where do you find delicious, easy-to-make recipes the rest of the family will eat without objection? The dieter or health-conscious person may be willing to accept uninspired, low-fat, low-sugar "diet" recipes—but what can you do when your kids want pizza and your husband insists on hot-fudge sundaes and pie?

Most diet recipes deserve their bad reputations. Too many of them sacrifice taste and appeal for lower calories and less sodium or sweetener. That's usually why nobody likes to eat them—and why even if we stick to this kind of eating for a while, we eventually jump off the wagon!

The *Healthy Exchanges® Cookbook* will change that—and change it for good. Ever since I began creating recipes, I aimed for what I call "common folk healthy"—meaning that the recipes I create have to fit into a busy lifestyle, they have to consider our family's likes and dislikes, and they have to appeal to everyone sitting at my table.

I do not shop at health-food stores, and I don't like preparing complicated dishes that keep me in the kitchen for hours. I got tired of being left with a pile of dirty dishes to show for all my efforts once the family had bolted from the table after ten minutes. If it takes longer to fix it than it does to eat it, forget it!

My goal is this: The foods that I prepare have to look, taste, smell, and feel like the foods we have always enjoyed. I have learned to "exchange" the excess fats and sugars within each recipe with readily available healthy ingredients, so we are still able to enjoy dishes like lasagna, potato salad, and banana-split pie. Besides reducing the overall fat and sugar content, I lowered the sodium content, too.

Using the *Healthy Exchanges® Cookbook* recipes can help you lose weight, lower and control your cholesterol and/or blood-sugar levels, and still allow you to enjoy delicious foods that deliver good nutrition and great "eye" appeal!

I didn't set out to impress anyone with fancy gourmet recipes that require unusual ingredients. Most of the mail I receive from people who've tried my recipes tells me that I made the right decision. They wanted (as my family and I did) to discover quick, tummy-pleasing, "common-folk" dishes that were healthy, too.

How did I come up with the concept for Healthy Exchanges®? I had three ideas in mind:

1. I wanted to "exchange" old, unhealthy habits for new, healthy ones in food, exercise, and mental attitude.

2. I chose to "exchange" ingredients within each recipe to eliminate as much fat and sugar as possible, while retaining the original flavor, appearance, and aroma.

3. I calculated all recipes using the exchange system of measuring daily food intake as established by the American Dietetic Association, the American Diabetic Association, and many national weight-loss organizations.

Next, before I included any recipe in the *Healthy Exchanges® Cookbook,* it had to meet my four "Musts." I knew that if I didn't address these "Musts" from the very beginning, I would be just dieting, and only days or minutes away from falling off the "health wagon" and into a binge where I would be keeping company again with cake donuts and hot-fudge sundaes (my personal favorites . . . and downfalls!).

By eliminating unnecessary preparation and excess "bad" foods, I've made it much easier to live and eat healthy. Each of my recipes must be:

1. *Healthy.* Every recipe is low in fat and sugar and within a reasonable range for sodium. And because they are all of these, they are also low in calories and cholesterol. The prepared food can be eaten with confidence by diabetics and heart patients as well as anyone interested in losing weight or maintaining a weight loss.

2. *Easy to make.* Most people don't have the time or the inclination for complicated recipes. They just want to prepare something quickly and get it on the table as fast as possible. But they still want their families to be smiling when they leave the table. Simply put, they want dishes that are quick and easy to prepare—but that don't look like it!

3. *As tasty and good as it looks.* If the foods we eat don't look, taste, smell, and feel like the family favorites we are used to eating, we won't be willing to eat them week in and week out.

   We are all creatures of habit. If we grew up eating fried chicken with mashed potatoes every Sunday at noon, we may try poached chicken with plain potatoes once—but we'll go running back to our favorite greasy chicken as soon as we can get our hands on some. However, if we could enjoy healthy yet delicious oven-fried chicken with healthy yet satisfying mashed potatoes topped with rich, thick, healthy gravy, we would probably agree to give up the deep-fried chicken dinner. Rather than demanding we give up a beloved comfort food, by serving a healthy version with all the great flavor of the original dish we remember, we can feel satisfied and willing to make this "Healthy Exchange®" for the rest of our lives.

   Here's another example. "Good enough" will never be good enough for me again. My food has to be garnished in easy yet attractive ways so I feed my eyes as well as my stomach. That's why I sprinkle one tablespoon of mini chocolate chips on top of my Triple-Layer Party Pie (see page 209). The pie serves eight, which works out to about ⅓ teaspoon of mini chips per person. But we definitely taste that crunch as we enjoy that piece of pie. And those delectable bites of real chocolate help keep us out of the chocolate chip package. It's when we think we can't have something that we dwell on it constantly until we do get it. Moderation is the cornerstone of Healthy Exchanges® recipes. My recipes include tiny amounts of mini chocolate chips, coconut, miniature marshmallows, nuts, and other foods I like to call "real-people" foods—not so-called "diet" foods. This is just one of the distinctions that sets my cookbook apart from others that emphasize low-fat and/or low-sugar foods.

4. *Made from ingredients found in DeWitt, Iowa.* If I can find the ingredients in a small town with a population of 4,500 in the middle of an Iowa cornfield, then anyone ought to be able to find them, no matter where they shop! To make these recipes, you do not have to drive to a specialty store in a large city, or visit a health-food store in search of special ingredients.

Once a recipe passes the four "Musts," I have a few additional requirements. The first requires using the entire can if the container has to be opened with a can opener. The reason for this is simple: only a few people are perfect Suzy and Homer Homemakers; most people are like me. If a recipe calls for ⅓ cup tomato sauce, I will put the rest in the refrigerator with good intentions to use it up within a day or two. Six weeks later I will probably have to toss it out because it got covered with moldly globs of green stuff. When I create a recipe, I devise a way to use the entire can and still have the dish taste delicious (and add up right when it comes to the mathematics of the exchanges for each serving).

Another requirement is what I call "Will It Play in Anytown, USA?" I ask myself if the retired person living on a meager pension or the young bride living on a modest paycheck can afford to prepare the recipe. I ask myself if the person with arthritic hands or the mother with two small children underfoot can physically manage to make the recipe. If the answers are yes, that recipe will be included in my cookbooks or newsletters.

It's important to me that my recipes are simple to make and understand. Here are some of the ways I do this:

- I provide both the closest cup or spoon measurement and the weight for each ingredient. Why? Well, everyone who follows the major diet plans or uses the American Diabetic Association program is required to use a kitchen scale every day. But I know that in the real world this just won't happen. People say they're too busy to pull the scale out of the cupboard. Or they'd rather not use the measuring bowl and have to wash it. So my recipe says that 3 ounces shredded reduced-fat cheese is equivalent to ¾ cup. I've measured this often to make sure it's right—why should you have to as well?

- I measure the final product and give the closest cup measurement per serving for anything that can't be cut into exact portions. For example, in a soup recipe, the serving size might be 1½ cups.

- I suggest baking all casseroles in an 8-by-8-inch pan for ease of portion control. If the dish serves 4, just cut it down the center, turn the dish, and cut it down the center again. Each cut square yields one serving. Many cookbooks call for a 1½-quart casserole, but I find that most people tend to scoop out too much or too little while the rest of the casserole collapses into the center. There's no guesswork my way—just an easy and accurate way to manage portion size.

The recipes in *Healthy Exchanges® Cookbook* are unique for another reason: they provide nutritional information calculated in three ways.

1. *Weight-Loss Choices™*. The recipes can be used by anyone attending the national weight-loss programs or support groups that count daily food intake by exchanges or selections instead of calories.

2. *Calories and Fat Grams*. I list the fat grams right next to the calories. In traditional recipes, fat grams usually appear in the middle of the nutrient information. Now, if a person chooses to count fat grams or compare the percentage of fat calories to total calories, the information is quickly found.

3. *Diabetic Exchanges.* A registered dietitian has calculated the diabetic exchanges to conform to the guidelines established by the American Diabetes Association. This makes *Healthy Exchanges*® *Cookbook* a wonderful resource for diabetics, for those who need to cook for diabetic family members, and for professionals who educate diabetics in how to eat healthfully and control their condition.

I've provided these three different kinds of nutritional measurements to make it easier for anyone and everyone to use my recipes as part of their commitment to a healthy lifestyle. I will do just about anything to make cooking healthier and easier for people—except do their dishes!

Are Healthy

Exchanges®

Recipes for You?

Do You Want to Lose Weight—and Keep It Off for Good?

I am living proof that you can lose weight while eating dishes prepared from Healthy Exchanges® recipes. I went from a much-too-tight size 28 to a healthy size 12 to 14 eating my own creations. I always make sure the bases are covered when it comes to meeting nutritional needs, and *then* I throw in tiny amounts of delicious treats—foods like miniature marshmallows that are usually considered "no-no's" in traditional diet recipes. Yes, we can get by without these little touches, but do we want to? Should we have to?

When I was a "professional" dieter, a typical lunch would consist of a couple of slices of diet bread, tuna packed in water, diet mayonnaise, lettuce, a glass of skim milk, and a small apple. Good healthy choices, all of them. But why was I always reaching for a candy bar or cake donuts just an hour later? Because I had fed only my stomach, and not my heart, my eyes, or my soul. It was only when I began enjoying a piece of a real dessert every day that I began to lose weight and keep it off permanently. This real dessert just happens to be low in calories, sugar, and fat! When I finally said NO to diets, I said YES to lasting weight loss!

The cardinal sin most people commit when going on a diet is to prepare two different meals—skimpy, get-the-weight-off-as-fastas-possible food for the dieter and real food for the rest of the family. My recipes can be eaten with confidence by anyone who wants to lose weight, but they are so tasty the entire family will gladly eat the same food. When you cook with Healthy Exchanges®, the burden of preparing two separate meals, not to mention the temptation of "sampling" the good stuff to be sure "it tastes right," has been eliminated. Now instead of short-term dieting and weight loss that never seems to last, you can take a step forward to healthy living for a lifetime!

Are You a Heart Disease Patient? Or Do You Just Need to Lower or Limit Cholesterol?

My Healthy Exchanges® recipes are all low in fat, just right for you if you're recovering from a heart attack or if you're trying to lower your cholesterol count. I have a recipe for Tamale Pie (see p. 155), for example, that calls for real ingredients and contains only 253 calories with 9 grams of fat per serving. It tastes just as good as a traditional recipe that delivers three times the amount of fat and almost twice the calories. And I don't skimp on the serving size! My approach provides a real savings in calories and fat without sacrificing flavor. While my own blood pressure and cholesterol levels are within the normal range, I know how important it is to eat a diet low in fat. My parents both died of heart disease, so I've always been concerned about fat intake. *Healthy Exchanges® Cookbook* provides dozens of delicious low-fat recipes to help you reach the best health possible.

Are You Diabetic? Do You Have Hypoglycemia?

My recipes are also low in sugar. A typical serving of Butterscotch-Raisin Meringue Pie prepared in the traditional way provides approximately 504 calories with 26 grams of fat per serving because processed sugar is the primary ingredient, and fat not too far behind. My recipe for this pie (see p. 204) is *208 calories per serving* with only 7 grams of fat—and just because I banished excess fats and sugars doesn't mean I've sacrificed any flavor. Besides, my pie can be cut into 8 pieces instead of the usual 12 servings per pie suggested in many diet recipes. With *Healthy Exchanges® Cookbook*, diabetic and hypoglycemic patients can find the "real world" desserts they've been missing. Again, while my own blood sugar is normal, both my parents and two uncles developed adult-onset diabetes. So creating delicious low-sugar recipes is a priority for me.

Are You Simply Interested in Preventing Medical Problems from Developing? Are You Ready to Make a Commitment to Eat Healthier?

Maybe you're lucky enough to have no immediate medical concerns, and you would like to keep it that way. Perhaps you've seen what the burdens of compromised health caused by a poor diet have been in family members or friends. You don't want to inherit the same "complications" you may have observed in parents and older family members, and you're determined to do your best to avoid future health problems by taking the necessary steps now. Healthy Exchanges® will help you ensure lifelong good health.

Are You Interested in Quick and Easy Recipes the Entire Family Will Love?

Maybe you don't really care if a recipe is healthy or not. Maybe you have other priorities right now in your life, and you don't want to spend any more time than necessary in the kitchen. But because you and your family have to eat, you want a collection of good-tasting dishes that can be "thrown together" without much fuss. *Healthy Exchanges® Cookbook* will give you recipes for healthy, delicious food that often can be prepared in five minutes or less. (Not including unattended cooking time, but that time is freed for other projects!)

Did you answer "yes" to any of those questions? If you did, then Healthy Exchanges® will give you just what you need—and deliciously, too!

Getting Started:
A Few Rules for
Success

A very important part of any journey is knowing where you are going and the best way to get there. If you plan and prepare before you start to cook, you should reach mealtime with foods worth bragging about!

1. Read the entire recipe from start to finish and be sure you understand the process involved. Check that you have all the equipment you will need *before* you begin.

2. Check the ingredient list and be sure you have *everything* and in the amounts required. Keep cooking sprays handy—while they're not listed as ingredients, I use them all the time (just a quick squirt!).

3. Set out all the ingredients and equipment needed to prepare the recipe on the counter near you *before* you start.

4. Do as much advance preparation as possible before actually cooking. Chop, cut, grate, or whatever is needed to prepare the ingredients and have them ready before you start to mix. Turn the oven on at least 10 minutes before putting food in to bake, to allow the oven to preheat to the proper temperature.

5. Use a kitchen timer to tell you when the cooking or baking time is up. Because stove temperatures vary slightly,

you may want to set your timer for 5 minutes less than the suggested time just to prevent overcooking. Check the progress of your dish at that time, then decide if you need the additional minutes or not.

6. Measure carefully. Use glass measures for liquids and metal or plastic cups for dry ingredients. My recipes are based on standard measurements. Unless I tell you it's a scant or full cup, measure the cup level.

7. For best results, follow the recipe instructions exactly. Feel free to substitute ingredients that *don't tamper* with the basic chemistry of the recipe, but be sure to leave key ingredients alone. For example, you could substitute sugar-free instant chocolate pudding for sugar-free butterscotch instant pudding, but if you used a 6-serving package when a 4-serving package was listed in the ingredients, or you used instant when cook-and-serve is required, you won't get the right result.

8. Clean up as you go. It is much easier to wash a few items at a time than to face a whole counterful of dirty dishes later. The same is true for spills on the counter or floor.

9. Be careful about doubling or halving a recipe. Though many recipes can be altered successfully to serve more or fewer people, many cannot. This is especially true when it comes to spices and liquids. If you try to double a recipe that calls for 1 teaspoon of pumpkin pie spice, for example, and you double the spice, you may end up with a too-spicy taste. I usually suggest increasing spices or liquid by 1½ times when doubling a recipe. You can always add more, but you can't take it out after it's stirred in.

10. Write your comments next to each recipe once you've tried it. Yes, that's right. I'm giving you permission to write in this book. It's yours, after all. Ask yourself: Did everyone like it? Did you have to add another half teaspoon of chili seasoning to please your family, who like to live on the spicier side of the street? You may even want to rate the recipe on a scale of 1 ★ to 4 ★, depending on

what you thought of it. (Four stars would be the top rating—and I hope you'll feel that way about many of my recipes.)

11. The brands suggested are my favorites *at this time*—carefully tested for taste, appearance, and ease of preparation—and are included only as suggestions. If you prefer another healthy brand, please feel free to substitute.

12. For canned goods, I've listed the most commonly found size. In most cases, if you can't find the exact size listed, use whatever can is closest in size, or two smaller cans that add up to the same number of ounces.

How to Read a

Healthy Exchanges®

Recipe

The Healthy Exchanges® Nutritional Analysis

Before using these recipes you may wish to consult your physician or health provider to be sure they are appropriate for you. The information in this book is not intended to take the place of any medical advice. It reflects my experiences, studies, research, and opinions regarding healthy eating.

Each recipe includes nutritional information calculated in three ways:

Healthy Exchanges®: Weight-Loss Choices™ or Exchanges (HE)

Calories and fat grams

Diabetic exchanges

In every Healthy Exchanges® recipe, the diabetic exchanges have been calculated by a registered dietitian. All the other calculations were done by computer, using the Food Processor II software. When the ingredient listing gives more than one choice, the first ingredient listed is the one used in the recipe analysis. Due to inevitable variations in the ingredients you choose to use, the nutritional values should be considered approximate.

The following abbreviations are used in each recipe's nutritional breakdown:

SM = Skim Milk   Ve = Vegetable
Fa = Fat   Pr = Protein
Br = Bread   Fr = Fruit
Sl = Slider™   OC = Optional Calories
St = Starch   Mt = Meat
Ca = Carbohydrate   So = Sodium
                        Fi = Fiber

The annotation "(limited)" following Protein counts in some recipes indicates that consumption of whole eggs should be limited to four per week.

Please note the following symbols:

☆ Read the recipe's directions carefully for special instructions about division of ingredients

❋ indicates FREEZES WELL

Healthy Exchanges®

Weight-Loss

Choices™/Exchanges

I f you've ever been on one of the national weight-loss programs like Weight Watchers or Diet Center, you've already been introduced to the concept of measured portions of different food groups that make up your daily food plan. If you are not familiar with such a system of weight-loss choices or exchanges, here's a brief explanation. (If you want or need more detailed information, you can write to the American Dietetic Association or the American Diabetes Association for comprehensive explanations.)

The idea of food exchanges is to divide foods into basic food groups. The foods in each group are measured in servings that have comparable values. These groups include Proteins/Meats, Breads/Starches, Vegetables, Fats, Fruits, Skim Milk, Free Foods, and Optional Calories.

Each choice or exchange included in a particular group has about the same number of calories and a similar carbohydrate, protein, and fat content as the other foods in that group. Because any food on a particular list can be "exchanged" for any other food in that group, it makes sense to call the food groups *exchanges* or *choices*.

I like to think we are also "exchanging" bad habits and food choices for good ones!

By using Weight-Loss Choices™ or exchanges you can choose from a variety of foods without having to calculate the nutrient value of each one. This makes it easier to include a wide variety of foods in your daily menus and gives you the opportunity to tailor your choices to your unique preferences.

If you want to lose weight, you should consult your physician or other weight-control expert regarding the number of servings that would be best for you from each food group. Since men generally require more calories than women, and since the requirements for growing children and teenagers differ from adults, the right number of exchanges for any one person is a personal decision.

I have included a suggested plan of weight-loss choices in the pages following the exchange lists. It's a program I used to lose 130 pounds, and it's the one I still follow today.

(If you are a diabetic or have been diagnosed with heart problems, consult your physician before using this or any other food program or recipe collection.)

Food Group Exchanges

Proteins (Pr)

Meat, poultry, seafood, eggs, cheese, and legumes. One exchange of Protein is approximately 60 calories. Examples of one protein choice or exchange:

1 ounce cooked weight of lean meat, poultry, or seafood
2 ounces white fish
1½ ounces 97% fat-free ham
1 egg
¼ cup egg substitute
3 egg whites
¾ ounce reduced-fat cheese
½ cup fat-free cottage cheese
2 ounces cooked or ¾ ounce uncooked dry beans

Breads (Br)

Breads, crackers, cereals, grains, and starchy vegetables. One exchange of Bread is approximately 80 calories. Examples of one bread choice or exchange:

1 slice bread or 2 slices reduced-calorie bread (40 calories or
    less)
1/2 cup cooked pasta or rice
3 tablespoons flour
3/4 ounce cereal
1/2 cup corn or peas

Fruits (Fr)

All fruits and fruit juices. One exchange of Fruit is approximately
60 calories. Examples of one Fruit choice or exchange:

1 small apple
1 small orange
1/2 medium banana
3/4 cup berries, except strawberries and cranberries
1 cup strawberries or cranberries
1/2 cup canned fruit, packed in fruit juice
2 tablespoons raisins
1 tablespoon spreadable fruit spread
1/2 cup apple juice

Skim Milk (SM)

Milk, buttermilk, and yogurt. One exchange of Skim Milk is
approximately 90 calories. Examples of one Skim Milk choice or
exchange:

1 cup skim milk
1/2 cup evaporated skim milk
1 cup low-fat buttermilk
3/4 cup plain fat-free yogurt
1/3 cup nonfat dry milk powder

Vegetables (Ve)

All fresh, canned, or frozen vegetables other than the starchy vegetables. One exchange of Vegetable is approximately 30 calories. Examples of one Vegetable choice or exchange:

½ cup vegetable
¼ cup tomato sauce
1 medium fresh tomato
½ cup vegetable juice

Fats (Fa)

Margarine, mayonnaise, vegetable oils, salad dressings, olives, and nuts. One exchange of Fat is approximately 40 calories. Examples of one Fat choice or exchange:

1 teaspoon margarine or 2 teaspoons reduced-calorie
  margarine
1 teaspoon vegetable oil
1 teaspoon mayonnaise or 2 teaspoons reduced-calorie
  mayonnaise
1 teaspoon peanut butter
1 ounce olives
¼ ounce pecans

Free Foods

Foods that do not provide nutritional value but are used to enhance the taste of foods are included in the Free Foods group. Examples of these are spices, herbs, extracts, vinegar, lemon juice, mustard, Worcestershire sauce, and soy sauce. Cooking sprays and artificial sweeteners used in moderation are also included in this group. However, you'll see that I include the caloric value of artificial sweeteners in the Optional Calories of the recipes.

You may occasionally see a recipe that lists "free food" as part of the portion. According to the published exchange lists, a free food contains fewer than 20 calories per serving. Two or three servings per day of free foods/drinks are usually allowed in a meal plan.

Optional Calories (OC)

Foods that do not fit into any other group but are used in moderation in recipes are included in Optional Calories. Foods that are counted in this way include sugar-free gelatin and puddings, fat-free mayonnaise and dressings, reduced-calorie whipped toppings, reduced-calorie syrups and jams, chocolate chips, coconut, and canned broth.

Sliders™ (Sl)

These are 80 Optional Calorie increments that do not fit into any particular category. You can choose which food group to *slide* it into. It is wise to limit this selection to a few times a week to ensure the best possible nutrition for your body while still enjoying an occasional treat.

Sliders™ may be used in either of the following ways:

1. If you have consumed all of your Proteins (Pr), Breads (Br), Fruit (Fr), or Skim Milk (SM) Weight-Loss Choices™ for the day, and you want to eat additional foods from those food groups, you simply use a Slider™ (Sl). It's what I call "healthy horse trading." Remember that Sliders™ may not be traded for choices in the Vegetables (Ve) or Fats (Fa) food groups.

2. Sliders™ may also be deducted from your Optional Calories (OC) for the day or week. ¼ Sl equals 20 OC; ½ Sl equals 40 OC; ¾ Sl equals 60 OC; and 1 Sl equals 80 OC. This way, you can choose the food group to *slide* it into. Use your Sliders™ to enjoy occasional treats, but it is wise to limit this choice to a total of five or six full Sliders™ each week to ensure the best possible nutrition for your body.

Healthy Exchanges®

Weight-Loss Choices™

H ere's my suggested program of Weight-Loss Choices™ for women, based on an average daily total of 1,400 to 1,600 calories. *If you require more or fewer calories, please revise this plan to your individual needs.*

Each day, you should plan to eat:

2 Skim Milk (SM) servings, 90 calories each

2 Fat (Fa) servings, 40 calories each

3 Fruit (Fr) servings, 60 calories each

4 or more Vegetable (Ve) servings , 30 calories each

5 Protein (Pr) servings, 60 calories each

5 Bread (Br) servings, 80 calories each

You may also choose to add up to 150 Optional Calories per day and up to 14 Sliders™ per week at 80 calories each. If you choose to include more Sliders™ in your daily or weekly totals, deduct those 80 calories from your Optional Calorie "bank."

A word about Sliders™: These are to be counted toward your totals after you have used your allotment of choices of Skim Milk, Protein, Bread, and Fruit for the day. By "sliding" an additional choice into one of these groups, you can meet your individual needs for that day. Sliders™ are especially helpful when traveling, stressed-out, eating out, or for special events. I often use mine so I can enjoy my favorite Healthy Exchanges® desserts. Vegetables are not to be counted as Sliders™. Enjoy as many Vegetable Choices as you need to feel satisfied. Because we want to limit our fat intake to moderate amounts, additional Fat choices should not be counted as Sliders™. If you choose to include more fat on an *occasional* basis, count the extra choices as Optional Calories.

Keep a daily food diary of your Weight-Loss Choices™, checking off what you eat as you go. If, at the end of the day, your required selections are not 100 percent accounted for, but you have done the best you can, go to bed with a clear conscience. There will be days when you have ¼ Fruit or ⅓ Protein left over. What are you going to do—eat two bites of an apple and throw the rest out? I always say that "nothing in life comes out exact." Just do the best you can . . . *the best you can.*

Try to drink at least 8 glasses of water a day. Water truly is the "nectar" of good health.

As a little added insurance, I take a multi-vitamin each day. It's not essential, but if my day's worth of well-planned meals "bites the dust" when unexpected events intrude on my regular routine, my body still gets its vital nutrients.

The calories listed in each group of choices are averages. Some choices within each group may be higher or lower, so it's important to select a variety of different foods instead of eating the same three or four all the time.

Use your Optional Calories (OC)! They are what I call "life's little extras." They make all the difference in how you enjoy your food and appreciate the variety available to you. Yes, we can get by without them, but do you really want to? Keep in mind that you should be using all your daily Weight-Loss Choices™ first to ensure you are getting the basics of good nutrition. But I guarantee that Optional Calories will keep you from feeling deprived—and help you reach your weight-loss goals.

Healthy Exchanges®

and Sodium

Most people consume more sodium than their bodies need. The American Heart Association and the American Diabetes Association recommend limiting daily sodium intake to no more than 3,000 milligrams per day. If your doctor suggests you limit your sodium even more, then *you really must read labels.*

Sodium is an essential nutrient and should not be completely eliminated. It helps to regulate blood volume and is needed for normal daily muscle and nerve functions. Most of us, however, have no trouble getting "all we need" and then some.

As with everything else, moderation is my approach. I rarely ever have salt in my list as an added ingredient. But if you're especially sodium-sensitive, make the right choices for you—and save high-sodium foods such as sauerkraut for an occasional treat.

I use lots of spices to enhance flavors, so you won't notice the absence of salt. In the few cases where it is used, it's vital for the success of the recipe, so please don't omit it.

When I do use an ingredient high in sodium, I try to compensate by using low-sodium products in the remainder of the recipe. Many fat-free products are a little higher in sodium to make up for any loss of flavor that disappeared along with the fat. But when I take advantage of these fat-free, higher-sodium products, I stretch that ingredient within the recipe, lowering the amount of sodium per serving. A good example is my use of fat-free canned soups. While the suggested number of servings per can is 2, I make sure my final creation serves at least four and sometimes six. So the soup's sodium has been "watered down" from one-third to one-half of the original amount.

Even if you don't have to watch your sodium intake for medical reasons, using moderation is another "healthy exchange" to make on your own journey to good health.

Healthy Exchanges®

and Fat Percentages

W e've been told that 30 percent is the magic number—that we should limit fat intake to 30 percent or less of our total calories. It's good advice, and I try to have a weekly average of 15 to 25 percent myself. I believe any less than 15 percent is really just another restrictive diet that won't last. And more than 25 percent on a regular basis is too much of a good thing.

When I started listing fat grams along with calories in my recipes, I was tempted to include the percentage of calories from fat. After all, in the vast majority of my recipes, that percentage is well below 30 percent. This even includes my pie recipes that allow you a realistic serving instead of many "diet" recipes that tell you a serving is $1/12$ of a pie.

Figuring fat grams is easy enough. Each gram of fat equals 9 calories. Multiply fat grams by 9, then divide that number by the total calories to get the percentage of calories from fat.

So why don't I do it? After consulting four registered dietitians for advice, I decided to omit this information. They felt that it's too easy for people to become obsessed by that 30 percent figure, which is, after all, supposed to be a percentage of total calories over the course of a day or a week. We mustn't feel we can't include a healthy ingredient *in moderation* such as pecans or olives in one recipe just because, on its own, it has more than 30 percent of its calories from fat.

An example of this would be a casserole made with 90 percent lean red meat. Most of us benefit from eating red meat in moderation, as it provides iron and niacin in our diets. If we *only* look at the percentage of calories from fat in a serving of this one dish, which might be as high as 40 to 45 percent, we might choose not to include this recipe in our weekly food plan.

The dietitians suggested that it's important to consider the total picture when making such decisions. As long as your overall food plan keeps fat calories to 30 percent, it's all right to enjoy an occasional dish that is somewhat higher in fat content. Healthy foods I include in moderation include 90 percent lean red meat, olives, and nuts. I don't eat these foods every day, and I know you don't either. But occasionally, in a good recipe, they make all the difference in the world between just getting by (deprivation) and truly enjoying your food.

Remember, the goal is eating in a healthy way so you can enjoy and live well the rest of your life.

Healthy Exchanges®

and Saturated Fats

and Cholesterol

Y ou'll see that I don't provide calculations for saturated fats or cholesterol amounts in my recipes. It's for the simple and yet not so simple reason that accurate, up-to-date, brand-specific information can be difficult to obtain from food manufacturers, especially since the way in which they produce food keeps changing rapidly. But once more I've consulted with registered dietitians and other professionals and found that because I use only a few products that are high in saturated fat, and use them in such limited quantities, my recipes are suitable for patients concerned about controlling or lowering cholesterol. You'll also find that whenever I do use one of these ingredients in moderation, everything else in the recipe, and in the meals my family and I enjoy, is low in fat.

Healthy Exchanges®
and Processed Foods

Some people have asked how "healthy" recipes can so often use "processed foods"—ready-made products like canned soups, prepared piecrusts, frozen potatoes, and frozen whipped topping. Well, I believe that such foods, used properly (that word *moderation* again) as part of a healthy lifestyle, have a place as ingredients in healthy recipes.

I'm not in favor of spraying everything we eat with chemicals, and I don't mean that all our foods should come out of packages. But I do think we should use the best available products to make cooking easier and foods taste better. I take advantage of good low-fat and low-sugar products, and my recipes are created for busy people like me who want to eat well and eat healthy. I don't expect people to visit out-of-the-way health-food stores or find time to cook beans from scratch—because I don't. There are lots of very good processed foods available in your local grocery store, and they can make it so much easier to enjoy the benefits of healthy eating.

Most of us can't grow fresh food in the backyard, and many people don't even have a nearby farmer's market. But instead of saying "Well, I can't get to the health-food store, so why not eat that hot-fudge sundae?" you gotta play ball where your ball field is. I want to help you figure out ways to make living healthy *manageable wherever you live,* or you're not going to stick with it.

Useful Healthy

Exchanges® Tips

and Tidbits

Measurements, General Cooking Tips, and Basic Ingredients

The word **moderation** best describes my use of **fats, sugar substitutes,** and **sodium** in these recipes. Wherever possible, I've used cooking spray for sautéing and for browning meats and vegetables. I also use reduced-calorie margarine and no-fat mayonnaise and salad dressings. Lean ground turkey *or* ground beef can be used in the recipes. Just be sure whatever you choose is at least *90 percent lean.*

I've also included **small amounts of sugar and brown-sugar substitutes as the sweetening agent** in many of the recipes. I don't drink a hundred cans of soda a day or eat enough artificially sweetened foods in a 24-hour time period to be troubled by sugar substitutes. But if this is a concern of yours and you *do not* need to watch your sugar intake, you can always replace the sugar substitutes with processed sugar and the sugar-free products with regular ones.

I created my recipes knowing they would also be used by hypoglycemics, diabetics, and those concerned about triglycerides. If you choose to use sugar instead, be sure to count the additional calories.

A word of caution when cooking with **sugar substitutes**: Use **saccharin**-based sweeteners when **heating** or **baking**. In recipes

33

that **don't require heat, Aspartame** (known as Nutrasweet) works well, but it leaves an aftertaste in baked products.

I'm often asked why I use an **8-by-8-inch baking dish** in my recipes. It's for portion control. If the recipe says it serves four, just cut down the center, turn the dish, and cut again. Like magic, there's your serving. Also, if this is the only recipe you are preparing requiring an oven, the square dish fits into a tabletop toaster oven easily—you save energy as you're saving calories.

To make life even easier, **whenever a recipe calls for ounce measurements** (other than raw meats) I've included the closest cup equivalent. I need to use my scale daily when creating recipes, so I've measured for you at the same time.

Most of the recipes are for **4 to 6 servings.** If you don't have that many to feed, do what I do: freeze individual portions. Then all you have to do is choose something from the freezer and take it to work for lunch or have your evening meals prepared in advance for the week. In this way, I always have something on hand that is both good to eat and good for me.

Unless a recipe includes hard-cooked eggs, cream cheese, mayonnaise, or a raw vegetable, **the leftovers should freeze well.** (I've marked recipes that freeze well with the symbol ✳. This includes most of the cream pies. Divide any recipe up into individual servings and freeze for your own "TV" dinners.

Unless I specify **"covered"** for simmering or baking, prepare my recipes **uncovered.** Occasionally you will read a recipe that asks you to cover a dish for a time, then to uncover, so read the directions carefully to avoid confusion—and to get the best results.

Low-fat cooking spray is another blessing in a Healthy Exchanges® kitchen. It's currently available in three flavors.

- Olive-Oil Flavored for cooking Mexican, Italian, or Greek dishes
- Butter Flavored when a hint of butter is desired
- Regular for everything else

A quick spray of butter-flavored spray makes air-popped popcorn a low-fat taste treat, or try it as a butter substitute on steaming hot corn on the cob. One light spray of the skillet when browning meat will convince you that you're using "old-fashioned fat," and a quick coating of the casserole dish before you add the ingredients will make serving easier and cleanup quicker.

I use reduced-sodium canned chicken broth in place of dry bouillon to lower the sodium content. The intended flavor is still present in the prepared dish. As a reduced-sodium beef broth is not currently available (at least not in DeWitt, IA), I use the canned regular beef broth. The sodium content is still lower than regular dry bouillon.

Whenever **cooked rice or pasta** is an ingredient, follow the package directions, but eliminate the salt and/or margarine called for. This helps lower the sodium and fat content. It tastes just fine; trust me on this.

Proteins

I use eggs in moderation. I enjoy the real thing on an average of three to four times a week. So, my recipes are calculated on using whole eggs. However, if you choose to use egg substitute in place of the egg, the finished product will turn out just fine and the fat grams per serving will be even lower than those listed.

If you like the look, taste, and feel of **hard-boiled eggs** in salads but haven't been using them because of the cholesterol in the yolk, I have a couple of alternatives for you: 1) Pour an 8-ounce carton of egg substitute into a medium skillet sprayed with cooking spray. Cover skillet tightly and cook over low heat until substitute is just set, about 10 minutes. Remove from heat and let sit, still covered, for 10 minutes more. Uncover and cool completely. Chop set mixture. This will make about 1 cup of chopped egg. 2) Even easier is to hard-boil "real eggs," toss the yolk away, and chop the white. Either way, you don't deprive yourself of the pleasure of egg in your salad.

In most recipes calling for **egg substitutes**, you can use 2 egg whites in place of the equivalent of 1 egg substitute. Just break the eggs open and toss the yolks away. I can hear some of you already saying, "But that's wasteful!" Well, take a look at the price on the egg substitute package (which usually has the equivalent of 4 eggs in it), then look at the price of a dozen eggs, from which you'd get the equivalent of 6 egg substitutes. Now, what's wasteful about that?

Whenever I include **cooked chicken** in a recipe, I use roasted white meat without skin. Whenever I include **roast beef or pork** in a recipe, I use the loin cuts because they are much leaner. However, most of the time, I do my roasting of all these meats at the local deli. I just ask for a chunk of their lean roasted meat, 6 or 8 ounces, and ask them not to slice it. When I get home, I cube or dice the meat and am ready to use it in my recipe. The reason I do this is three-fold: (1) I'm getting just the amount I need without leftovers; (2) I don't have the expense of heating the oven; and (3) I'm not throwing away the bone, gristle, and fat I'd be cutting away from the meat. Overall, it is probably cheaper to "roast" it the way I do.

Did you know that you can make an acceptable meat loaf without using egg for the binding? Just replace every egg with ¼ cup of liquid. You could use beef broth, tomato sauce, even applesauce, to name just a few. For a meat loaf to serve 6, I always use 1 pound of extra-lean ground beef or turkey, 6 tablespoons of dried fine bread crumbs, and ¼ cup of the liquid, plus anything else healthy that strikes my fancy at the time. I mix well and place the mixture in an 8-by-8-inch baking dish or 9-by-5-inch loaf pan sprayed with cooking spray. Bake uncovered at 350 degrees for 35 to 50 minutes (depending on the added ingredients). You will never miss the egg.

Anytime you are **browning ground meat** for a casserole and want to get rid of almost all the excess fat, just place the uncooked meat loosely in a plastic colander. Set the colander in a glass pie plate. Place in microwave and cook on HIGH for 3 to 6 minutes (depending on the amount being browned), stirring often. Use as you would for any casserole. You can also chop up onions and cook them with the meat if you want.

Milk and Yogurt

Take it from me—nonfat dry milk powder is great! I *do not* use it for drinking, but I *do* use it for cooking. Three good reasons why:

1. It is very *inexpensive.*

2. It does not *sour* because you use it only as needed. Store the box in your refrigerator or freezer and it will keep almost forever.

3. You can easily *add extra calcium* to just about any recipe without added liquid.

I consider nonfat dry milk powder one of the modern-day miracles of convenience.

In many of my pies and puddings, I use nonfat dry milk powder and water instead of skim milk. Usually I call for ⅔ cup nonfat dry milk powder and 1¼ to 1½ cups water or liquid. This way I can get the nutrients of two cups of milk, but with less liquid, and the end result is much creamier. Also, the recipe sets faster, usually in 5 minutes or less. So if someone knocks at your door unexpectedly at mealtime, you can quickly throw a pie together and enjoy it minutes later.

You can make your own "sour cream" by combining ¾ cup plain fat-free yogurt with ⅓ cup nonfat dry milk powder. The dry milk stabilizes the yogurt and keeps the whey from separating. The dry milk helps to cut the tartness of the yogurt. It's still virtually fat-free and the calcium has been increased by 100 percent. Isn't it great how we can make that distant relative of sour cream a first kissin' cousin by adding the nonfat dry milk powder? Or, if you place 1 cup of plain fat-free yogurt in a sieve lined with a coffee filter, and place the sieve over a small bowl and refrigerate for about 6 hours, you will end up with a very good alternative for sour cream. To **stabilize yogurt** when cooking or baking with it, just add 1 teaspoon cornstarch to every ¾ cup yogurt.

If a recipe calls for **evaporated skim milk** and you don't have any in the cupboard, make your own. For every ½ cup evaporated skim milk needed, combine ⅓ cup nonfat dry milk powder and ½ cup water. Use as you would evaporated skim milk.

You can also make your own **sugar-free and fat-free sweetened condensed milk** at home. Combine 1⅓ cups nonfat dry milk powder and ½ cup cold water in a 2-cup glass measure. Cover and microwave on HIGH until mixture is hot but *not* boiling. Stir in ½ cup Sprinkle Sweet or Sugar Twin. Cover and refrigerate for at least 4 hours. This mixture will keep for up to two weeks in the refrigerator. Use in just about any recipe that calls for sweetened condensed milk.

Fruits and Vegetables

If you want to enjoy a **"fruit shake"** with some pizazz, just combine soda water and unsweetened fruit juice in a blender. Add crushed ice. Blend on HIGH until thick. Refreshment without guilt.

You'll see that many recipes use ordinary **canned vegetables.** They're much cheaper than reduced-sodium versions, and once you rinse and drain them, the sodium is reduced anyway. I believe in saving money wherever possible so we can afford the best fat-free and sugar-free products as they come onto the market.

All three kinds of **vegetables—fresh, frozen, and canned—** have their place in a healthy diet. My husband, Cliff, hates the taste of frozen or fresh green beans, thinks the texture is all wrong, so I use canned green beans instead. In this case, canned vegetables have their proper place when I'm feeding my husband. If someone in your family has a similar concern, it's important to respond to it so everyone can be happy and enjoy the meal.

When I use fruits or vegetables like apples, cucumbers, and zucchini, I wash them really well and **leave the skin on**. It provides added color, fiber, and attractiveness to any dish. And, because I use processed flour in my cooking, I like to increase the fiber in my diet by eating my fruits and vegetables in their closest-to-natural state.

The next time you warm canned vegetables such as carrots or green beans, drain and heat the vegetables in ¼ cup beef or chicken broth. It makes a nice variation of an old standby. Here's a simple white sauce for vegetables and casseroles that doesn't add fat: Spray a medium saucepan with butter-flavored cooking spray. Combine 1½ cups evaporated skim milk and 3 tablespoons flour in a covered jar. Shake well. Pour into the saucepan and cook over medium heat until thick, stirring constantly. Add salt and pepper to taste. You can also add ½ cup canned drained mushrooms and/or 3 ounces (¾ cup) shredded reduced-fat cheese. Continue cooking until cheese melts.

Zip up canned or frozen green beans with chunky salsa: ½ cup salsa to 2 cups beans. Chunky salsa also makes a wonderful dressing on lettuce salads. It only counts as a vegetable, so enjoy.

For gravy with that "old-time" flavor but without the extra fat, try this almost effortless way to prepare it. (It's almost as easy as opening up a store-bought jar.) Pour the juice off your roasted meat, then set the roast aside to "rest" for about 20 minutes. Place the juice in an uncovered cake pan or other large flat pan (we want the large air surface to speed up the cooling process) and put it in the freezer until the fat congeals on top and you can skim it off— about the same 20 minutes it takes for the roast to rest. Or, if you prefer, use a skimming pitcher purchased at your kitchen gadget store. Either way, measure about 1½ cups skimmed juice and pour into a medium saucepan. Cook over medium heat until heated through, about 5 minutes. In a covered jar, combine ½ cup water or cooled potato broth with 3 tablespoons flour. Shake well. Pour flour mixture into the warmed juice. Combine well using a wire whisk. Continue cooking until gravy thickens, about 5 minutes. Season with salt and pepper to taste.

Why did I use flour instead of cornstarch? Because any leftovers will reheat nicely with the flour base and would not with a cornstarch base. Also, 3 tablespoons of flour works out to 1 Bread/Starch exchange. This virtually fat-free gravy makes about 2 cups, so you could spoon about ½ cup of gravy on your low-fat mashed potatoes and only have to count your gravy as ¼ Bread/Starch exchange.

Desserts

Thaw lite whipped topping in the refrigerator overnight. Never try to force the thawing by stirring or using a microwave to soften. Stirring it will remove the air from the topping that gives it the lightness and texture we want, and there's not enough fat in it to survive being heated.

How can I frost an entire pie with just ½ cup of whipped topping? First, don't use an inexpensive brand. I use Cool Whip Lite or La Creme Lite. Make sure the topping is fully thawed. Always spread from the center to the sides using a rubber spatula. This way, ½ cup topping will literally cover an entire pie. Remember, the operative word is *frost*. Don't pile the entire container on top of the pie!

Here's a way to enhance and extend whipped topping without adding fat. Blend together ¾ cup plain nonfat yogurt and ⅓ cup nonfat dry milk powder. Add sugar substitute to equal 2 tablespoons sugar, 1 cup Cool Whip Lite, and 1 teaspoon of the flavoring of your choice (vanilla, coconut, or almond are all good choices). Gently mix and use as you would whipped topping. The texture is almost a cross between marshmallow cream and whipped cream. This is enough to mound high on a pie.

For a different taste when preparing sugar-free instant pudding mixes, use ¾ cup plain nonfat yogurt for one of the required cups of milk. Blend as usual. It will be *thicker and creamier*. And, it doesn't taste like yogurt. Another variation for preparing the sugar-free instant vanilla pudding is to use 1 cup skim milk and 1 cup crushed pineapple juice. Mix as usual.

For a special treat that tastes anything but "diet," try placing **spreadable fruit** in a container and microwave for about 15 seconds. Then pour the melted fruit spread over a serving of nonfat ice cream or frozen yogurt. One tablespoon of spreadable fruit is equal to 1 fruit serving. Some combinations to get you started are apricot over chocolate ice cream, strawberry over strawberry ice cream, or any flavor over vanilla.

The next time you are making baked treats for the family, try using **unsweetened applesauce** for some or all the required oil in the recipe. For instance, if the recipe calls for ½ cup cooking oil, use applesauce instead. It works and most people will not even notice the difference. It's great in purchased cake mixes, but so far I haven't been able to figure out a way to deep-fat fry with it!

Another trick I often use is to include tiny amounts of "real people" food, such as coconut, but extend the flavor by using extracts. Try it—you will be surprised by how little of the real thing you can use and still feel you are not being deprived.

If you are preparing a pie filling that has ample moisture such as prepared pudding mix, just line the bottom of a 9-by-9-inch cake pan with **graham crackers**. Pour the filling over the top of the crackers. Cover and refrigerate until the moisture has enough time to soften the crackers. Overnight is best. This eliminates the added **fats and sugars of a piecrust.**

Many of my pie recipes can be frozen (always check for the symbol to be sure) but it's best to cut the leftover pie into individual servings and place each in individual Ziploc bags before you place them in the freezer. That way, when you need one piece, you can pull only one out instead of thawing the entire pie. If you freeze and thaw a pie more than once, you could end up with a disappointing dessert!

When **stirring fat-free cream cheese to soften it,** use only a sturdy spoon, never an electric mixer. The speed of a mixer can cause the cream cheese to lose its texture and become watery.

Did you know you can make your own **fruit-flavored yogurt?** Mix 1 tablespoon of any flavor of spreadable fruit spread with ¾ cup plain yogurt. It's every bit as tasty and much cheaper. You can also make your own **lemon yogurt** by combining 3 cups plain fat-free yogurt with 1 tub Crystal Light lemonade powder. Mix well, cover, and store in the refrigerator. I think you will be pleasantly surprised by the ease, cost, and flavor of this "made from scratch" calcium-rich treat. You can make any flavor you like by using any of the Crystal Light mixes—Cranberry? Iced tea? You decide.

Sugar-free puddings and gelatins are important to many of my recipes, but if you prefer to avoid sugar substitutes, you could still prepare the recipes with regular puddings or gelatins. The calories would be higher, but you would still be cooking low-fat.

When a recipe calls for **chopped nuts** (and you only have whole ones), who wants to dirty the food processor just for a couple of tablespoons? You could try to chop them using your cutting board, but be prepared for bits and pieces to fly all over the kitchen. I use "Grandma's food processor." I use the biggest nuts I can find, put them in a small glass bowl, and chop them into chunks just the right size using a metal biscuit cutter.

If you have a **leftover muffin** and are looking for something a little different for breakfast, you can make a "breakfast sundae." Crumble the muffin into a cereal bowl. Sprinkle a serving of fresh fruit over it and top with a couple of tablespoons of nonfat plain yogurt sweetened with sugar substitute and your choice of extract.

The thought of it just might make you jump out of bed with a smile on your face. (Speaking of muffins, did you know that if you fill the unused muffin wells with water when baking muffins, you help ensure more even baking and protect the muffin pan at the same time?)

The secret of making **good meringues** without sugar is to use 1 tablespoon of Sprinkle Sweet or Sugar Twin for every egg white, and ½ to 1 teaspoon extract per batch. Almond, vanilla, and coconut are all good choices. Use the same amount of cream of tartar you usually do. Bake the meringue in the usual way. Don't think you can't have meringue pies because you can't eat sugar. You can, if you do it my way. (Remember that egg whites whip up best at room temperature.)

A Peek into My Pantry and My Favorite Brands

I 've been asked many times what types of foods I keep on hand and what brands I use. There are lots of good products on the grocery shelves today—many more than we dreamed about even one year ago. And I can't wait to see what's out there twelve months from now. The following are my staples and, where appropriate, my favorites *at this time*. I feel these products are healthier, tastier, easy to get—and deliver the most flavor for the least amount of fat, sugar, or calories. If you find others you like as well *or better*, use them. This is only a guide to make your grocery shopping and cooking easier.

Fat-free plain yogurt (*Yoplait*)

Nonfat dry skim milk powder (*Carnation*)

Evaporated skim milk (*Carnation*)

Skim milk

Fat-free cottage cheese

Fat-free cream cheese (*Philadelphia*)

Fat-free mayonnaise (*Kraft*)

Fat-free salad dressings (*Kraft*)

Fat-free sour cream (*Land O Lakes*)

Reduced-calorie margarine (*Weight Watchers, Smart Beat, or Promise*)

Cooking spray:

Butterflavored *(Weight Watchers)*

Olive oil–flavored and regular *(Pam)*

Vegetable oil *(Puritan Canola Oil)*

Reduced-calorie whipped topping *(Cool Whip Lite or La Creme Lite)*

Sugar substitute:

if no heating is involved *(Equal)*

if heating is required—

white *(Sprinkle Sweet or Sugar Twin)*

brown *(Brown Sugar Twin)*

Sugar-free gelatin and pudding mixes *(Jell-O)*

Baking mix *(Bisquick Reduced-Fat)*

Pancake mix *(Hungry Jack Extra Lights or Aunt Jemima Lite)*

Reduced-calorie syrup *(Cary's Reduced-Calorie Maple)*

Parmesan cheese *(Kraft's Grated House Italian Cheese)*

Reduced-fat cheese *(Kraft, Healthy Favorites, or Weight Watchers)*

Shredded frozen potatoes *(Mr. Dell's)*

Spreadable fruit *(Smucker's, Welch's, or Sorrell Ridge)*

Peanut butter *(Peter Pan Reduced-Fat, Jif Reduced-Fat, or Skippy Reduced-Fat)*

Chicken broth *(Campbell's Healthy Request)*

Beef broth *(Swanson)*

Tomato sauce *(Hunt's—Regular and Chunky)*

Canned soups *(Campbell's Healthy Request)*

Tomato juice *(Campbell's Healthy Request)*

Ketchup *(Campbell's Healthy Request or Heinz Lite)*

Purchased piecrust:

unbaked *(Pillsbury—from dairy case)*

graham cracker, butterflavored, or chocolate flavored *(Keebler)*

90 percent lean pastrami or corned beef (*Carl Buddig*)

Luncheon meats (*Healthy Choice*)

97 percent fat-free reduced-sodium ham (*Dubuque*)

Lean frankfurters and Polish kielbasa sausage (*Healthy Choice*)

Canned white chicken, packed in water (*Swanson*)

90 percent lean ground turkey

90 percent lean ground beef

Canned tuna, packed in water (*Starkist*)

Soda crackers (*Nabisco Fat-Free Premium*)

Reduced-calorie bread—40 calories per slice or less (*Colonial or Wonder Bread*)

Hamburger buns—80 calories each (*Colonial Old Fashion*)

Rice—instant, regular, brown, and wild

Instant potato flakes (*Betty Crocker Potato Buds*)

Noodles, spaghetti, and macaroni

Salsa (*Chi Chi's Mild*)

Pickle relish—dill, sweet, and hot dog

Mustard—Dijon, prepared, and spicy

Unsweetened apple juice

Unsweetened applesauce

Frozen fruit—no sugar added

Fresh fruit

Fresh, frozen, and canned vegetables

Spices

Lemon and lime juice

Instant fruit beverage mixes (*Crystal Light*)

Dry dairy beverage mixes (*Alba, Nestlé's Quik, and Swiss Miss*)

"Ice Cream" (*Well's Blue Bunny Fat-Free and Sugar-Free Dairy Dessert, Weight Watchers*)

If your grocer does not stock these items, why not ask if they can be ordered on a trial basis? If the store agrees to do so, be sure to tell your friends to stop by, so that sales are good enough to warrant shelf space for the new products.

The items on my shopping list are normal, everyday foods, but as low-fat and low-sugar (while still tasting good) as I can find. I can make any recipe in this cookbook as long as these staples are on my shelves. After using the products for a couple of weeks, you will find it becomes routine to have them on hand. And I promise you, I DON'T spend any more at the store now than I did a few years ago when I told myself I couldn't afford some of these items. Back then, of course, plenty of unhealthy, high-priced snacks I really DIDN'T need somehow made the magic leap from the grocery shelves into my cart. Who was I kidding?

The Healthy
Exchanges® Kitchen

If you ever come to DeWitt, Iowa, and visit the Lunds, I can already guess your reaction when you first see my kitchen. You'll be surprised to discover I don't have a massive test kitchen stocked with every modern appliance and handy gadget ever made. When you take a look at my tiny galley kitchen that has room for only one person at a time, I bet you'll echo the comment I get most often: "Oh, my! You mean all those recipes were created in this tiny kitchen?" Yes, it's true.

Because storage is at such a premium in my "test kitchen," I don't waste space with equipment I don't really need. Here's a list of what I consider worth having. If you notice serious gaps in your equipment, you can probably find most of what you need at a local discount store or garage sale. If your kitchen is equipped with more sophisticated appliances, use them. Enjoy every appliance you can find room for or that you can afford. Just be assured that healthy, quick, and delicious food can be prepared with the "basics."

A Healthy Exchanges® Kitchen Equipment List

Good-quality nonstick skillets (medium, large)

Good-quality saucepans (small, medium, large)

Glass mixing bowls (small, medium, large)

Glass measures (1-cup, 2-cup, 4-cup, 8-cup)

Sharp knives (paring, chef, butcher)

Rubber spatulas	4-inch round custard dishes
Wire whisks	Glass pie plates
Measuring spoons	8-by-8-inch glass baking dishes
Measuring cups	Cake pans (9-by-9-, 9-by-13-inch)
Large mixing spoons	10¾-by-7-by-1½-inch biscuit
Egg separator	pan
Covered jar	Cookie sheets (good nonstick ones)
Vegetable parer	Jelly-roll pan
Grater	Muffin tins
Potato masher	5-by-9-inch bread pan
Electric mixer	Plastic colander
Electric blender	Cutting board
Electric skillet	Pie wedge server

Slow cooker   Square-shaped server

Air popper for popcorn   Can opener (I prefer manual)

Cooking timer   Rolling pin

Kitchen scales (unless you *always* use my recipes)

Wire racks for cooling baked goods

Electric toaster oven (to conserve energy for those times when
    only one item is being baked or for a recipe that requires a
    short baking time)

Making Healthy Exchanges® Work for You

Y ou're ready now to begin a wonderful journey to better health. In these pages, you'll discover the remarkable variety of good food available to you when you begin eating the Healthy Exchanges® way. You'll stock your pantry and learn many of my food preparation "secrets" that will point you on the way to delicious success.

Before you jump into the recipes, I'd like to share a few tips that I've learned while traveling toward healthier eating habits. It took me a long time to learn how to eat *smarter*. In fact, I'm still working on it. But I am getting better. For years, I could *inhale* a five-course meal in five minutes flat—and still make room for a second helping of dessert!

Now I follow certain signposts on the road that help me stay on the right path. I hope these ideas will help point you in the right direction as well.

1. **Eat slowly** so your brain has time to catch up with your tummy. Cut and chew each bite slowly. Try putting your fork down between bites. Stop eating as soon as you feel full. Crumple up your napkin and throw it on top of your plate so you don't continue to eat when you are no longer hungry.

2. **Smaller plates** may help you feel more satisfied by your food portions *and* limit the amount you can put on the plate.

3. **Watch portion size.** If you are *truly* hungry, you can always add more food to your plate once you've finished your initial serving. But remember to count the additional food accordingly.

4. **Always eat at your dining-room or kitchen table.** You deserve better than nibbling from an open refrigerator or over the sink. Make an attractive place setting, even if you're eating alone. Feed your eyes as well as your stomach. By always eating at a table, you will become much more aware of your true food intake. For some reason, many of us conveniently "forget" the food we swallow while standing over the stove, munching in the car or on the run.

5. **Avoid doing anything else while you are eating.** If you read the paper or watch television while you eat, it's easy to consume too much food without realizing it, because you are concentrating on something else besides what you're eating. Then, when you look down at your plate and see that it's empty, you wonder where all the food went and why you still feel hungry.

Day by day, as you travel the path to good health, it will become easier to make the right choices, to eat *smarter*. But don't ever fool yourself into thinking that you'll be able to put your eating habits on cruise control and forget about them. Making a commitment to eat good, healthy food and sticking to it takes some effort. But with all the good-tasting recipes in this *Healthy Exchanges® Cookbook,* just think how well you're going to eat—and enjoy it—from now on!

Healthy lean bon appétit!

JoAnn

The Healthy
Exchanges® Recipes

Soups

L ots of people have come up to me and said, "I love soup, but I have no time to make it from scratch." Very few people do. But I'm going to show you it's possible to make delicious, healthy, and hearty soup dishes in just a few minutes, with only a couple of easy steps. In most recipes, I begin with the best available canned reduced-fat or fat-free soups and add just the right ingredients to create satisfying, good-tasting soups that will surprise you with their flavor and creamy goodness. Soups can be an important part of a healthy eating plan, perfect for quick lunches or late suppers all year round. Accompanied by a sandwich or salad, my Healthy Exchanges® soups will convince you that you've had a meal!

Basic Vegetable Soup

This soup will help to fill the empty spots in your tummy. Keep it on hand in the fridge for those unexpected hunger attacks.

○ Serves 8 (1½ cups)

> 4 cups (two 16-ounce cans) canned tomatoes with juice
> 3½ cups (two 14½- ounce cans) canned beef broth
> 4 cups coarsely chopped cabbage
> 2 cups chopped celery
> 2 cups chopped carrots
> 1 cup chopped onion
> 2 tablespoons lemon juice
> 1 tablespoon Sprinkle Sweet or Sugar Twin

Blend tomatoes in blender on CHOP for 10 seconds. In a large saucepan, combine blended tomatoes and beef broth. Add cabbage, celery, carrots, onion, lemon juice, and Sprinkle Sweet. Lower heat. Cover and simmer 2 hours.

Hint: The lemon juice helps your system digest all those nutritious vegetables.

Each serving equals:
HE: 3¼ Ve, 10 OC
61 Calories, 1 gm Fa, 3 gm Pr, 11 gm Ca, 613 mg So, 2 Fi
DIABETIC: 2 Ve

French Cabbage Soup

If you like cabbage, this soup is sure to become a regular at your house. That unglamorous vegetable shines like the star it is in this tummy-warming soup. ☻   Serves 6 (1½ cups)

> 4 cups (one 32-fluid-ounce bottle) canned mixed vegetable
>   juice
> 1¾ cups (one 14½-ounce can) canned beef broth
> 1 package dry onion soup mix
> 1 cup sliced celery
> 3 cups shredded cabbage
> 1 cup diced onion

In a large saucepan, combine vegetable juice, beef broth, and dry onion soup mix. Add celery, cabbage, and onion. Lower heat, cover, and simmer 1 hour.

Each serving equals:

HE: 3 Ve, ¼ Sl, 6 OC
64 Calories, 0 gm Fa, 2 gm Pr, 13 gm Ca, 969 mg So, 2 Fi
DIABETIC: 2 Ve, 1 Free Ve

Almost Instant Gazpacho

I once heard someone call gazpacho "a garden in a glass," which is a pretty good description of the flavors in this quick and refreshing cold soup. Even if your garden is the local supermarket's produce patch, enjoy! ❍   Serves 4 (1 cup)

> 1 (10³/4-ounce) can Campbell's Healthy Request Tomato
>   Soup
> 1 cup water
> 2 tablespoons Kraft fat-free Italian dressing
> 1¼ cups chopped cucumber
> 1½ cups chopped fresh tomato
> ¼ cup chopped green bell pepper
> ¼ teaspoon minced garlic
> 1 teaspoon dried onion flakes

In a medium bowl, combine tomato soup, water, and Italian dressing. Add cucumber, tomato, green pepper, garlic, and onion flakes. Mix well. Cover and refrigerate until ready to serve.

Each serving equals:

HE: 1½ Ve, ½ Sl, 5 OC

89 Calories, 2 gm Fa, 1 gm Pr, 17 gm Ca, 373 mg So, 2 Fi

DIABETIC: 1 St or 3 Ve

Cheese-Vegetable Chowder

Here's a great way to ensure that you get your vitamins! Unless you've tasted the vegetables in this delicious cheesy base, you may not believe me when I tell you that this low-fat soup is as satisfying and good as any high-fat soup in the land.

● Serves 4 (1½ cups)

> 2 cups (one 16-ounce can) Campbell's Healthy Request
>   Chicken Broth
> 1 cup sliced carrots
> ½ cup chopped celery
> ½ cup chopped onion
> 2 cups skim milk
> 3 tablespoons flour
> 1 scant cup (3¾ ounces) Kraft shredded reduced-fat
>   Cheddar cheese
> 1 teaspoon dried parsley flakes
> ⅛ teaspoon black pepper

In a medium saucepan, combine chicken broth, carrots, celery, and onion. Bring mixture to a boil. Reduce heat and simmer until vegetables are tender. In a covered jar, combine milk and flour. Shake well. Pour into broth mixture. Add Cheddar cheese, parsley flakes, and black pepper. Continue cooking until thick and bubbly, stirring often.

Each serving equals:

HE: 1¼ Pr, 1 Ve, ½ SM, ¼ Br, 8 OC

160 Calories, 4 gm Fa, 14 gm Pr, 17 gm Ca, 528 mg So, 2 Fi

DIABETIC: 2 Ve, 1 Mt, ½ SM

Cream of Tomato and Rice Soup ❄

If you think you can't make a cream soup without cream, cook up a pot of this thick soup—then see what you think! Your family will never know. ● Serves 4 (1½ cups)

4 cups (two 16- ounce cans) canned tomatoes with juice
1¾ cups (one 14½- ounce can) canned beef broth
¼ cup water
1 cup Carnation nonfat dry milk powder
2 cups cooked rice
¼ teaspoon black pepper
1 teaspoon dried parsley flakes

Place tomatoes in blender container. Process on CHOP for 10 seconds. In a large saucepan, combine beef broth, water, and dry milk powder. Mix well using a wire whisk. Stir in chopped tomatoes, rice, black pepper, and parsley flakes. Cook over medium heat until heated through.

Hint: 1⅓ cups dry rice usually make 2 cups cooked.

Each serving equals:

HE: 2 Ve, ¾ SM, 1 Br, 9 OC

202 Calories, 1 gm Fa, 12 gm Pr, 36 gm Ca, 862 mg So, 2 Fi

DIABETIC: 1 Ve, 1 SM, 1 St

Tomato-Mushroom Soup

So elegant, yet so quick to prepare. This may be just what you are looking for to start a meal for company.

○ Serves 4 (1¼ cups)

2 teaspoons reduced-calorie margarine
½ cup chopped onion
½ teaspoon dried minced garlic or 1 clove garlic, minced
2 cups sliced fresh mushrooms
2 cups (one 16-ounce can) Campbell's Healthy Request Chicken Broth
1¾ cups (one 15-ounce can) Hunt's Chunky Tomato Sauce
¼ teaspoon lemon pepper
¼ cup (¾ ounce) grated Kraft House Italian or Parmesan cheese
2 teaspoons dried parsley flakes

In a medium saucepan, melt margarine. Add onion and garlic. Sauté until onion is tender. Add mushrooms and continue to sauté 2 to 3 minutes. Stir in chicken broth, tomato sauce, and lemon pepper. Cover. Lower heat and simmer 20 minutes. To serve, pour into individual soup bowls. Sprinkle each serving with 1 tablespoon House Italian cheese and ½ teaspoon parsley flakes.

Each serving equals:

HE: 3 Ve, ¼ Fa, ¼ Pr, 8 OC
108 Calories, 4 gm Fa, 6 gm Pr, 12 gm Ca, 948 mg So, 3 Fi
DIABETIC: 2 Ve, 1 Free Ve, ½ Mt

Swiss Potato Soup

This creamy delight can stand alone for a soothing lunch on a cold day, or couple it with a low-fat ham sandwich for a filling late-night supper. ❍ Serves 4 (1¼ cups)

1 10¾-ounce can Campbell's Healthy Request Cream of
  Mushroom Soup
2 cups skim milk
1½ cups (8 ounces) diced cooked potatoes
⅛ teaspoon black pepper
¼ teaspoon dry mustard or ½ teaspoon prepared mustard
5(¾-ounce) slices Weight Watchers reduced-fat Swiss
  cheese, shredded
2 teaspoons chopped parsley

In a medium saucepan, combine mushroom soup, skim milk, potatoes, black pepper, and mustard. Cook over medium heat until potatoes are warmed through. Add Swiss cheese and parsley. Continue cooking until cheese melts, stirring often.

Each serving equals:

HE: 1¼ Pr, ½ Br, ½ SM, ½ Sl, 1 OC
218 Calories, 8 gm Fa, 11 gm Pr, 25 gm Ca, 794 mg So, 1 Fi
DIABETIC: 1½ St, 1 Mt, ½ SM

Spanish Corn Soup

Olé! Olé! Olé! Bring on this tasty soup anytime you want to score a "bull's-eye" with your family. (If you like spicy foods as much as my husband, Cliff, does, increase the seasoning . . . a little at a time.) ☻ Serves 4 (1½ cups)

> 2 cups (one 16-ounce can) Campbell's Healthy Request
> Chicken Broth
> ½ cup chopped onion
> 1 scant cup (4 ounces) diced cooked chicken breast
> 2 cups (one 16-ounce can) canned tomatoes with juice,
> chopped
> 2 cups frozen whole-kernel corn
> ½ teaspoon minced garlic
> 1 teaspoon chili seasoning mix
> ⅛ teaspoon black pepper

In a large saucepan, combine chicken broth and onion. Cook over low heat until onion is tender, about 5 minutes. Add chicken, tomatoes, corn, garlic, chili seasoning, and black pepper. Lower heat. Cover and simmer 20 minutes.

Hints: 1. Purchase a chunk of cooked chicken breast from your local deli and dice it when you get home.
2. Packaged chili seasoning mixes, such as McCormick or Shilling, have more flavor than just plain chili powder.

Each serving equals:

HE: 1¼ Ve, 1 Pr, 1 Br, 8 OC
161 Calories, 2 gm Fa, 14 gm Pr, 22 gm Ca, 464 mg So, 2 Fi
DIABETIC: 1 Ve, 1 Mt, 1 St

Midwest Corn Chowder

This soup just says "Welcome" in aroma, taste, and appearance. The evaporated skim milk gives you the texture of cream without the fat, and the chicken and corn combine for a rich and flavorful "main-course" soup. ☻ Serves 4 (1½ cups)

> 4 cups (two 16-ounce cans) Campbell's Healthy Request
>   Chicken Broth
> 2 cups frozen whole-kernel corn
> 1 cup (5 ounces) diced cooked chicken breast
> ½ cup (one 2.5-ounce jar) canned sliced mushrooms,
>   drained
> 1 tablespoon dried onion flakes
> 1 teaspoon dried parsley flakes
> ⅛ teaspoon black pepper
> 1½ cups (one 12-fluid-ounce can) Carnation evaporated
>   skim milk
> 3 tablespoons flour

In a medium saucepan, combine chicken broth, corn, chicken, mushrooms, onion flakes, parsley flakes, and black pepper. Bring mixture to a boil. Reduce heat and simmer about 15 minutes. In a covered jar combine evaporated skim milk and flour. Shake well. Pour into hot soup mixture. Stir well. Lower heat and simmer 10 minutes, stirring often.

Each serving equals:

HE: 1¼ Br, 1¼ Pr, ¾ SM, ¼ Ve, 8 OC
236 Calories, 2 gm Fa, 23 gm Pr, 32 gm Ca, 466 mg So, 1 Fi
DIABETIC: 1½ St, 1 Mt, 1 SM

Chicken-Corn Chowder

Farmhouse taste no matter where you live. The cream-style corn, coupled with the evaporated skim milk, makes this my candidate for the creamiest low-fat soup ever! ● Serves 4 (1½ cups)

2 cups (one 16-ounce can) Campbell's Healthy Request
   Chicken Broth
1 cup (5 ounces) diced raw potatoes
1 cup diced carrots
2 cups (one 16-ounce can) cream-style corn
1½ cups (8 ounces) diced cooked chicken breast
1½ cups (one 12-fluid-ounce can) Carnation evaporated
   skim milk
⅛ teaspoon black pepper
⅓ cup (¾ ounce) instant potato flakes
1 teaspoon dried parsley flakes

In a large saucepan, combine chicken broth, potatoes, and carrots. Cover and cook over medium heat until vegetables are tender, about 10 to 12 minutes. Add cream-style corn, chicken, evaporated skim milk, and black pepper. Stir in instant potato flakes and parsley flakes. Simmer 5 minutes.

Each serving equals:

HE: 2 Pr, 1½ Br, ¾ SM, ½ Ve, 8 OC
325 Calories, 3 gm Fa, 30 gm Pr, 47 gm Ca, 773 mg So, 2 Fi
DIABETIC: 2 Mt, 2 St, 1 SM, ½ Ve

Chicken-Cabbage-Noodle Soup

I love cabbage, and I love the "comfort" feeling of noodles. You might not think of these two—chicken and cabbage—teamed up together with noodles, but this trio is dynamite.

● Serves 6 (1½ cups)

> 4 cups (two 16-ounce cans) Campbell's Healthy Request
>   Chicken Broth
> 1½ cups (8 ounces) diced cooked chicken breast
> 2 cups finely shredded cabbage
> 1 cup finely shredded carrots
> ½ cup diced onion
> ½ cup diced celery
> 1 scant cup (1½ ounces) uncooked medium-width noodles
> 1 tablespoon reduced-sodium soy sauce
> ⅛ teaspoon pepper
> 1 teaspoon dried parsley flakes

In a large saucepan, combine chicken broth, diced chicken, cabbage, carrots, onion, and celery. Bring mixture to a boil. Reduce heat. Add noodles, soy sauce, pepper, and parsley. Continue simmering, covered, until vegetables and noodles are tender, about 20 minutes.

Each serving equals:

HE: 2½ Ve, 2 Pr, ½ Br, 16 OC

130 calories, 2 gm Fa, 16 gm Pr, 12 gm Ca, 369 mg So, 2 Fi

DIABETIC: 1½ Mt, 1 St, 1 Free Ve

Savory Salads

W hen you hear the word salad, do you immediately think of plain lettuce and tomato, served dry, with a small dish of diet dressing on the side? Too many people who want to lose weight or eat healthy seem to believe they have no choice but to eat such a boring dish while everyone else enjoys tangy coleslaws, spirited entrée salads, and spicy vegetable combinations tossed with delicious dressings. Good news! In this section you'll discover that Healthy Exchanges® salads invite you to join the party, with simple-to-prepare recipes for all those "real-people" salads—and more. Once you explore the possibilities, you'll have dozens of new salads to share with family and friends.

Creamy Cucumbers

This is my daughter Becky's all-time favorite cucumber salad—and its creamy base comes from a bottle of fat-free dressing. Isn't it great that we've lost the fat—but not the great taste?

○ Serves 4 (1 full cup)

> 4 cups sliced cucumbers
> ½ cup sliced white onion
> ½ cup Kraft fat-free Ranch dressing
> ¼ teaspoon salt
> ⅛ teaspoon black pepper

In a large bowl, combine cucumbers and onions. Pour Ranch dressing over cucumbers and onions. Add salt and black pepper. Stir gently to combine. Cover and refrigerate for at least 2 hours.

Each serving equals:

HE: 2¼ Ve, ½ Sl, 10 OC

71 Calories, 0 gm Fa, 1 gm Pr, 16 gm Ca, 446 mg So, 1 Fi

DIABETIC: 2 Ve

Mike's Cucumber Salad

When our friend Michael brought me a big bag full of fresh cucumbers, I tried to think of a new way to prepare them that both Mike and my husband, Cliff, would enjoy. You'll see I was right on target with the addition of salsa—one with lots of chunks of onion, tomato, and peppers. ☻ Serves 6 (¾ cup)

> 3½ cups sliced cucumbers
> ½ cup chopped white onion
> 1 cup chunky salsa
> ⅓ cup Kraft fat-free Ranch dressing
> ¼ cup Kraft fat-free mayonnaise
> 1 teaspoon parsley flakes

In a medium bowl, combine cucumbers and onion. In a small bowl, combine salsa, Ranch dressing, mayonnaise, and parsley flakes. Pour over cucumber mixture. Toss gently to combine. Cover and refrigerate until ready to serve. Stir gently before serving.

Each serving equals:

HE: 1⅔ Ve, ¼ Sl, 9 OC

52 Calories, 0 gm Fa, 1 gm Pr, 12 gm Ca, 374 mg So, 1 Fi

DIABETIC: 2 Ve

French Cucumber Salad

This is just about as easy a cucumber salad as you are ever going to find. Best of all, it doesn't "taste easy."

○   Serves 4 (¾ cup)

¼ cup Kraft fat-free French dressing
1 tablespoon Kraft fat-free mayonnaise
2 tablespoons chopped fresh parsley or 1 teaspoon dried
  parsley flakes
2¼ cups thinly sliced cucumbers
¼ cup finely chopped white onion

In a medium bowl, combine French dressing, mayonnaise, and parsley. Add cucumbers and onion. Toss gently to combine. Cover and refrigerate until ready to serve.

Each serving equals:

HE: 1¼ Ve, ¼ Sl, 10 OC
29 Calories, 0 gm Fa, 0 gm Pr, 7 gm Ca, 148 mg So, 1 Fi
DIABETIC: 1 Ve

Tomatoes 'n' Cream

Once you try this tangy combination of flavors, you'll never eat just plain sliced tomatoes again. You could even experiment with other fat-free dressings for a taste-bud buffet of tomato salads.

● Serves 4 (¾ cup)

> 2 cups coarsely chopped fresh tomatoes
> ½ cup chopped Bermuda onion
> ¼ cup Kraft fat-free Ranch dressing

In a medium bowl, combine tomatoes and onion. Pour Ranch dressing over tomato mixture. Stir gently to combine. Cover and refrigerate for at least 2 hours.

Each serving equals:

HE: 1¼ Ve, ¼ Sl, 5 OC

45 Calories, 0 gm Fa, 1 gm Pr, 10 gm Ca, 159 mg So, 1 Fi

DIABETIC: 2 Ve

Creamy Italian Tomato Salad

Plain tomatoes will never be the same after you sample this tasty salad. It's very refreshing on a hot summer night at the height of tomato season. But then again, it's also great on a cold winter night. Take your pick! ☻   Serves 4 (full ⅔ cup)

> 2 cups cherry tomatoes, quartered
> 3 tablespoons (¾ ounce) Kraft shredded reduced-fat
>   mozzarella cheese
> ¼ cup Kraft fat-free Ranch dressing
> 2 tablespoons Kraft fat-free Italian dressing
> 1 tablespoon fresh parsley or 1 teaspoon dried parsley flakes

In a medium bowl, combine tomatoes and mozzarella cheese. In a small bowl, combine Ranch dressing and Italian dressing. Mix well. Pour dressing over tomatoes. Add parsley. Mix gently to combine. Cover and refrigerate for at least 15 minutes. Mix gently before serving.

Each serving equals:

HE: 1 Ve, ¼ Pr, ¼ Sl, 7 OC

57 Calories, 1 gm Fa, 2 gm Pr, 10 gm Ca, 289 mg So, 1 Fi

DIABETIC: 2 Ve, ½ Fa

Carrot Salad

Most carrot salads are sweet, but you'll discover that adding a dash of horseradish to this colorful, crunchy vegetable provides a great new taste sensation. ☻ Serves 4 (¾ cup)

2³/4 cups grated carrots
½ cup chopped celery
¼ cup chopped green bell pepper
¼ cup Kraft fat-free mayonnaise
1 tablespoon white vinegar
Sugar substitute to equal 2 teaspoons sugar
1 teaspoon prepared horseradish

In a medium bowl, combine carrots, celery, and green pepper. In a small bowl, combine mayonnaise, vinegar, sugar substitute, and horseradish. Pour over carrot mixture. Mix well to combine. Cover and refrigerate for at least 1 hour.

Each serving equals:

HE: 1³/4 Ve, 9 OC

48 Calories, 0 gm Fa, 1 gm Pr, 11 gm Ca, 166 mg So, 2 Fi

DIABETIC: 2 Ve

Green Bean–Carrot Salad

I know that you know that green beans and carrots are supposed to be good for you. But this salad combo will make you shout from the rooftops that they're good-tasting too!

● Serves 8 (²⁄₃ cup)

> 2 cups (one 16-ounce can) canned green beans, rinsed and drained
> 2 cups (one 16-ounce can) canned sliced carrots, rinsed and drained
> ¼ cup thinly sliced white onion
> ¼ cup chopped green bell pepper
> ½ cup chopped celery
> 2 tablespoons snipped fresh parsley
> ⅓ cup white vinegar
> Sugar substitute to equal 4 teaspoons sugar
> 4 teaspoons vegetable oil
> ½ teaspoon dry mustard or 1 teaspoon prepared mustard
> ¼ teaspoon lemon pepper

In a medium bowl, combine green beans, carrots, onion, green pepper, celery, and parsley. In covered jar combine vinegar, sugar substitute, vegetable oil, mustard, and lemon pepper. Shake well. Pour mixture over vegetables. Stir to coat. Cover and refrigerate for several hours.

Each serving equals:

HE: 1¼ Ve, ½ Fa, 2 OC

42 Calories, 2 gm Fa, 1 gm Pr, 5 gm Ca, 180 mg So, 1 Fi

DIABETIC: 1 Ve, ½ Fa

Cabbage and Carrot Salad

This is my basic cabbage salad, without any added fats or sugars. You've heard that it's smart to "get back to basics"—now here's an appetizing way to do it! ❂ Serves 2 (1 cup)

1 teaspoon vinegar
¼ cup Kraft fat-free mayonnaise
Sugar substitute to equal 1 teaspoon sugar
¼ teaspoon salt
⅛ teaspoon black pepper
2 cups shredded cabbage
½ cup shredded carrots

In a large bowl, combine vinegar, mayonnaise, sugar substitute, salt, and black pepper. Add cabbage and carrots. Mix well to combine. Cover and refrigerate for at least 1 hour.

Each serving equals:

HE: 2½ Ve, 17 OC
54 Calories, 0 gm Fa, 1 gm Pr, 13 gm Ca, 539 mg So, 2 Fi
DIABETIC: 2 Ve

Carrot-Apple Salad

Adding apples and apple-pie spice to a traditional carrot and raisin salad gives it more than just crunch—it gives it a whole new flavor! ❂ Serves 4 (¾ cup)

2 cups shredded carrots
1 cup unpeeled apples, cored and chopped (2 small)
¼ cup raisins
2 tablespoons (½ ounce) chopped pecans
⅓ cup Kraft fat-free mayonnaise
Sugar substitute to equal 2 teaspoons sugar
½ teaspoon apple-pie spice
1 teaspoon lemon juice

In a medium bowl, combine carrots, apples, raisins, and pecans. Add mayonnaise, sugar substitute, apple-pie spice, and lemon juice. Toss lightly to combine. Cover and refrigerate for at least 1 hour.

Hints: 1. You can use ¼ teaspoon cinnamon, ⅛ teaspoon nutmeg, and ⅛ teaspoon ginger instead of apple-pie spice. But the already blended purchased apple-pie spice is quicker, easier, and tastier!
2. To plump up raisins without "cooking," place in glass measuring cup and microwave on HIGH for 15 seconds.

Each serving equals:
HE: 1 Ve, 1 Fr, ½ Fa, 12 OC
124 Calories, 3 gm Fa, 1 gm Pr, 24 gm Ca, 186 mg So, 3 Fi
DIABETIC: 1 Ve, 1 Fr, 1 Fa

Spinach Salad

Attractive enough for "party fare," this classic is tasty enough for family meals. Even Popeye would approve of this salad.

● Serves 4 (1⅓ cups)

> 4 cups fresh torn spinach, stems discarded
> 1 hard-boiled egg, chopped
> 2 tablespoons Hormel Bacon Bits
> 1 cup fresh sliced mushrooms
> ½ cup Kraft fat-free French dressing
> 1 tablespoon finely chopped white onion
> ½ teaspoon Worcestershire sauce
> 1 tablespoon Brown Sugar Twin

In a medium bowl, combine spinach, chopped egg, bacon bits, and mushrooms. In a small bowl combine French dressing, onion, Worcestershire sauce, and Brown Sugar Twin. Add to spinach mixture. Toss well to coat.

Hint: Fresh spinach needs to be rinsed thoroughly to get rid of the sand. Spin or pat dry; remove and discard coarse stems.

Each serving equals:

HE: 2½ Ve, ¼ Pr (limited), ½ Sl, 13 OC
92 Calories, 2 gm Fa, 5 gm Pr, 13 gm Ca, 302 mg So, 2 Fi
DIABETIC: 2 Ve, ½ Mt

Calico Coleslaw

Tired of the same old coleslaw? Well, this is one salad that will make any meal a party. The peas, bacon bits, and Parmesan cheese give this easy dish its calico appearance . . . and lots of tangy flavor. ☉   Serves 8 (¾ cup)

> 4 cups shredded cabbage
> 1½ cups shredded carrots
> ½ cup diced white onion
> 1 cup frozen peas, thawed
> ¼ cup Hormel Bacon Bits
> ½ cup (1½ ounces) grated Kraft House Italian or Parmesan
>   cheese
> 1 cup Kraft fat-free mayonnaise
> Sugar substitute to equal 1 tablespoon sugar
> ⅛ teaspoon lemon pepper

In a large bowl, combine cabbage, carrots, onions, peas, bacon bits, and House Italian cheese. In a small bowl, combine mayonnaise, sugar substitute, and lemon pepper. Pour mayonnaise mixture over cabbage. Mix well. Cover and refrigerate for several hours.

Each serving equals:

HE: 1½ Ve, ¼ Br, ¼ Pr, ¼ Sl, 12 OC
161 Calories, 6 gm Fa, 11 gm Pr, 16 gm Ca, 701 mg So, 2 Fi
DIABETIC: 2 Ve, 1 Free Ve, 1 Fa, ½ Mt

Mustard Coleslaw

After tasting this winning combination of Dijon mustard and cabbage, you will never be satisfied with "plain" coleslaw again.

○ Serves 6 (¾ cup)

4 cups purchased coleslaw mix

1 cup finely chopped celery

1 tablespoon dried parsley flakes

½ cup Kraft fat-free mayonnaise

1 tablespoon white vinegar

Sugar substitute to equal 2 tablespoons sugar

1 tablespoon Dijon mustard

⅛ teaspoon black pepper

In a large bowl, combine coleslaw mix and celery. In a small bowl, combine parsley flakes, mayonnaise, vinegar, sugar substitute, Dijon mustard, and black pepper. Add to vegetables. Mix gently to combine. Cover and refrigerate until ready to serve.

Hint: 3½ cups shredded cabbage and ½ cup shredded carrots can be used in place of purchased coleslaw mix.

Each serving equals:

HE: 1⅓ Ve, 13 OC

36 Calories, 0 gm Fa, 1 gm Pr, 8 gm Ca, 243 mg So, 1 Fi

DIABETIC: 1 Ve, 1 Free Ve

Pineapple Coleslaw

Here's a tropical treat—a coleslaw that combines pineapple and green bell pepper for a fresh new taste. My son James is the coleslaw expert in the family, and he gives this version two thumbs up! ☻   Serves 2 (1 cup)

2 cups shredded cabbage
¼ cup chopped green bell pepper
¼ cup chopped celery
1 tablespoon dried onion flakes
1 cup (one 8-ounce can) canned pineapple chunks, packed in
*   their own juice (drained)*
¼ cup white vinegar
Sugar substitute to equal 1 tablespoon sugar

In a medium bowl, combine cabbage, green pepper, celery, onion flakes, and pineapple chunks. In a small bowl, combine vinegar and sugar substitute. Add to cabbage mixture. Toss well to combine. Cover and refrigerate for at least 2 hours before serving.

Each serving equals:
HE: 2½ Ve, 1 Fr, 3 OC
118 Calories, 0 gm Fa, 2 gm Pr, 28 gm Ca, 16 mg So, 2 Fi
DIABETIC: 2 Ve, 1 Fr

Amana Coleslaw

I created this dish when a woman traveling through Iowa on vacation asked me to re-create the salad she had enjoyed at our world-famous Iowa Amana Colonies, an Amish community renowned for great home cooking. I did—and she loved it. Best of all, my tasty version is fat-free! ☻   Serves 6 (⅔ cup)

3½ cups shredded cabbage
¾ cup shredded carrots
½ cup finely diced celery
¼ cup finely diced white onion
½ cup Kraft fat-free mayonnaise
¼ teaspoon lemon pepper
2 teaspoons prepared horseradish
Sugar substitute to equal 2 tablespoons sugar
1 tablespoon white vinegar
1 teaspoon celery seed

In a medium bowl, combine cabbage, carrots, celery, and onion. In a small bowl, combine mayonnaise, lemon pepper, horseradish, sugar substitute, vinegar, and celery seed. Add to cabbage mixture. Mix well to combine. Cover and refrigerate for at least 1 hour.

Each serving equals:

HE: 1⅔ Ve, 18 OC
39 Calories, 0 gm Fa, 1 gm Pr, 9 gm Ca, 191 mg So, 1 Fi
DIABETIC: 1 Ve, 1 Free Ve

Waldorf Coleslaw

You don't have to dine at the Waldorf-Astoria hotel in New York City to enjoy the varied flavors of this eye- and tummy-pleasing salad. A traditional Waldorf salad includes apples and nuts in a creamy dressing, but this one delivers a classic taste with almost none of the fat and calories of the original!

● Serves 8 (¾ cup)

> 4 cups shredded cabbage
> 1 cup unpeeled apples, cored and chopped (2 small)
> ½ cup raisins
> ½ cup (2 ounces) chopped dry-roasted peanuts
> ¾ cup plain fat-free yogurt
> ⅓ cup Carnation nonfat dry milk powder
> ½ cup Kraft fat-free mayonnaise
> Sugar substitute to equal 1 tablespoon sugar

In a large bowl, combine cabbage, apples, raisins, and peanuts. In a small bowl, combine yogurt and dry milk powder. Add mayonnaise and sugar substitute. Mix well. Blend into cabbage. Toss lightly. Cover and refrigerate for several hours before serving.

Hint: To plump up raisins without "cooking," place in glass measuring cup and microwave on HIGH for 30 seconds.

Each serving equals:

HE: 1 Ve, ¾ Fr, ½ Fa, ¼ Pr, ¼ SM, 9 OC

133 Calories, 4 gm Fa, 5 gm Pr, 20 gm Ca, 165 mg So, 2 Fi

DIABETIC: 1 Fr, 1 Ve, 1 Fa

Kidney Bean Salad

This favorite of the '50s makes a perfect '90s dish—with a few healthy adjustments. Kidney beans are filling, a good low-cost protein, and easy to prepare. What more could you ask?

◐   Serves 8 (½ cup)

> 20 ounces (two 16-ounce cans) canned red kidney beans,
>   rinsed and drained
> 2 hard-boiled eggs, chopped
> 1 cup celery, chopped
> ½ cup Kraft fat-free Ranch dressing
> ⅛ teaspoon black pepper

In a large bowl, combine kidney beans, chopped eggs, and celery. Add Ranch dressing and black pepper. Mix well to combine. Cover and refrigerate.

Hint: To lower the fat grams even more, discard the egg yolks and use only the egg whites.

Each serving equals:

HE: 1½ Pr (¼ limited), ¼ Ve, ¼ Sl, 5 OC

94 Calories, 2 gm Fa, 5 gm Pr, 14 gm Ca, 184 mg So, 3 Fi

DIABETIC: 1 Mt, 1 St

Mexican Corn Salad

Combining terrific eye appeal and a bit of South-of-the-Border flavor, this creamy corn salad is a good side dish for a Sunday night chili supper. ❂ Serves 4 (⅔ cup)

> 2 cups (one 16-ounce can) canned whole-kernel corn, rinsed and drained
> ¼ cup chopped white onion
> ¼ cup chopped green bell pepper
> ¼ cup (1 ounce) sliced pimiento-stuffed green olives
> ¼ cup Kraft fat-free mayonnaise
> 1 teaspoon chili seasoning mix
> ¼ teaspoon salt
> ⅛ teaspoon black pepper

In a medium bowl, combine corn, onion, green pepper, and olives. In a small bowl, combine mayonnaise, chili seasoning mix, salt, and black pepper. Blend into corn mixture. Cover and refrigerate for at least 2 hours.

Each serving equals:

HE: 1 Br, ¼ Ve, ¼ Fa, 8 OC

91 Calories, 1 gm Fa, 2 gm Pr, 19 gm Ca, 569 mg So, 2 Fi

DIABETIC: 1 St

Deviled Lettuce

Your family will call you an angel when you serve them this heavenly salad. The combination of ham, cream cheese, and lettuce is unexpected—and unbelievably good!

● Serves 8 (1 cup)

6 cups shredded lettuce
½ cup chopped celery
¼ cup chopped green bell pepper
¼ cup chopped white onion
1 (8-ounce) package Philadelphia fat-free cream cheese
½ cup Kraft fat-free mayonnaise
1 full cup (6 ounces) finely diced Dubuque 97% fat-free or
* any extra-lean ham*
1 tablespoon prepared mustard
1 tablespoon Brown Sugar Twin

In a large bowl, combine lettuce, celery, green pepper, and onion. Layer on bottom of large low-sided serving bowl. In a medium bowl, stir cream cheese with spoon until soft. Add mayonnaise, ham, mustard, and Brown Sugar Twin. Drop cream cheese mixture by spoonfuls on top of lettuce. Cover and refrigerate for at least 2 hours. Toss just before serving.

Each serving equals:
HE: 1¾ Ve, 1 Pr, 8 OC
67 Calories, 1 gm Fa, 8 gm Pr, 6 gm Ca, 511 mg So, 1 Fi
DIABETIC: 1 Ve, 1 Mt

Dijon Chicken Salad

This is a wonderful way to use up any leftover chicken (and don't you always have a piece or two lurking in the fridge?). It also makes a great lunchbox sandwich, and a nice change from plain old chicken. If you don't have leftovers, purchase a chunk of cooked chicken breast from your local deli.

○ Serves 2 (½ cup)

> 2 tablespoons Kraft fat-free mayonnaise
> 2 teaspoons Dijon mustard
> 1 tablespoon finely chopped onion
> 1 scant cup (4 ounces) diced cooked chicken breast
> ⅛ teaspoon lemon pepper

In a medium bowl, combine mayonnaise, mustard, and onion. Add chicken and lemon pepper. Toss gently to combine. Serve on lettuce as a salad or use as a sandwich filling.

Each serving equals:

HE: 2 Pr, 8 OC

111 Calories, 3 gm Fa, 18 gm Pr, 3 gm Ca, 339 mg So, 0 Fi

DIABETIC: 2 Mt

Almond Chicken Salad

This combination of chicken and almonds definitely seems like destiny. If there were ever a perfect pair, it's these elegant nuts blended with healthy poultry chunks for an easy-to-prepare, delicious-to-eat salad to serve your best friends.

⊙   Serves 4 (½ cup)

> 1 full cup (6 ounces) diced cooked chicken breast
> ¼ cup (1 ounce) toasted slivered almonds
> ½ cup chopped celery
> ⅓ cup Kraft fat-free mayonnaise
> 1 tablespoon lemon juice
> 1 tablespoon chopped fresh parsley or 1 teaspoon dried
>   parsley flakes
> ¼ teaspoon salt
> ⅛ teaspoon black pepper

In a medium bowl, combine chicken, almonds, and celery. In a small bowl, combine mayonnaise, lemon juice, parsley, salt, and black pepper. Blend into chicken mixture and toss lightly. Refrigerate until ready to serve.

Each serving equals:

HE: 1¾ Pr, ½ Fa, ¼ Ve, 11 OC

129 Calories, 5 gm Fa, 15 gm Pr, 6 gm Ca, 403 mg So, 1 Fi

DIABETIC: 2 Mt

Chicken Waldorf Salad

What a refreshing way to serve chicken! Even those most suspicious of "diet foods" will love this potpourri of flavors—and they'll ask for seconds. ☻   Serves 2 (¾ cup)

> 1 scant cup (4 ounces) diced cooked chicken breast
> ½ cup red unpeeled apple, cored and diced (1 small)
> ½ cup chopped celery
> 2 tablespoons raisins
> ¼ cup Kraft fat-free mayonnaise

In a small bowl, combine chicken, apple, celery, and raisins. Blend in mayonnaise. Refrigerate until ready to serve. When serving, spoon onto lettuce leaf.

Hint: To plump up raisins without "cooking," place in glass measuring cup and microwave on HIGH for 15 seconds.

Each serving equals:

HE: 2 Pr, 1 Fr, ¼ Ve, 16 OC

191 Calories, 2 gm Fa, 18 gm Pr, 25 gm Ca, 407 mg So, 2 Fi

DIABETIC: 2 Mt, 1 Fr, ½ St

Ham and Pea Salad

Both my husband, Cliff, and son Tommy can't get enough of this flavorful main-dish salad. I think it's the addition of the prepared mustard that gives it that special taste. ❂ Serves 4 (½ cup)

2 cups frozen peas, thawed
½ cup (3 ounces) finely chopped Dubuque 97% fat-free or
   any extra-lean ham
1 hard-boiled egg, chopped
⅓ cup (1½ ounces) Kraft shredded reduced-fat Cheddar
   cheese
¼ cup Kraft fat-free Ranch dressing
1 tablespoon Kraft fat-free mayonnaise
1 teaspoon prepared mustard
⅛ teaspoon black pepper

In a medium bowl, combine peas, ham, egg, and Cheddar cheese. In a small bowl, combine Ranch dressing, mayonnaise, mustard, and black pepper. Pour over pea mixture. Mix gently to combine.

Hint: Thaw peas by placing in a colander and rinsing under hot water for one minute.

Each serving equals:
   HE: 1¼ Pr (¼ limited), 1 Br, ¼ Sl, 8 OC
   152 Calories, 4 gm Fa, 12 gm Pr, 17 gm Ca, 556 mg So, 3 Fi
   DIABETIC: 1 St, 1 Mt

Polynesian Salad

You don't have to travel to the South Seas to savor this mouthwatering main-dish salad. But if you're already packed, I won't stop you. Just promise to send me a postcard.

○ Serves 8 (1 cup)

> *1 tablespoon + 1 teaspoon reduced-calorie margarine*
> *2 tablespoons Brown Sugar Twin*
> *1 full cup (6 ounces) diced Dubuque 97% fat-free or any*
>   *extra-lean ham*
> *4 cups cooked elbow macaroni, rinsed and drained*
> *2 cups (two 8-ounce cans) canned pineapple chunks, packed*
>   *in their own juice, drained; reserve 2 tablespoons juice*
> *³/₄ cup (3 ounces) Kraft shredded reduced-fat Cheddar or*
>   *American cheese*
> *¹/₂ cup chopped green bell pepper*
> *¹/₂ cup Kraft fat-free mayonnaise*
> *³/₄ cup plain fat-free yogurt*
> *¹/₃ cup Carnation nonfat dry milk powder*
> *¹/₂ teaspoon salt*

In a large skillet, melt margarine with Brown Sugar Twin; add diced ham. Cook and stir until ham is golden brown. Cool. In a large bowl, combine macaroni, pineapple, cheese, and green pepper. In a small bowl, combine mayonnaise, yogurt, dry milk powder, reserved pineapple juice, and salt. Stir into macaroni mixture. Blend in cooled ham mixture. Refrigerate for at least 2 hours.

Hint: 3 cups dry elbow macaroni usually make about 4 cups cooked.

Each serving equals:

HE: 1 Br, 1 Pr, ¹/₂ Fr, ¹/₄ Fa, ¹/₄ SM, 10 OC

227 Calories, 3 gm Fa, 12 gm Pr, 37 gm Ca, 609 mg So, 1 Fi

DIABETIC: 1¹/₂ St, 1 Fr, 1 Mt

Italian Kidney Bean Salad

If you like kidney beans and pasta, you will love this quick salad. Besides the fact that it tastes good, you'll see that the color combination is "food for the eyes." ☻ Serves 6 (¾ cup)

2 cups cooked rotini pasta
1 cup frozen peas, thawed
10 ounces (one 16-ounce can) canned red kidney beans,
   rinsed and drained
1 hard-boiled egg, chopped
½ cup Kraft fat-free Italian dressing

In a medium bowl, combine rotini pasta, peas, kidney beans, and chopped egg. Add Italian dressing and mix gently to combine. Cover and refrigerate until ready to serve.

Hint: 1½ cups uncooked rotini pasta usually make about 2 cups cooked.

Each serving equals:

HE: 1 Br, 1 Pr, 5 OC

161 Calories, 1 gm Fa, 9 gm Pr, 29 gm Ca, 225 mg So, 2 Fi

DIABETIC: 1½ St, ½ Pr

Cliff's Macaroni-Pea Salad

When I was creating this recipe, I realized I was using many of my husband Cliff's favorite foods. So, when he tried it and liked it, I told him I'd name it for him. He beamed for days and couldn't stop telling everyone how good it was. Try it and let Cliff know what you think. ☻   Serves 6 (1 full cup)

2 cups cooked elbow macaroni, rinsed and drained
1 cup frozen peas, thawed
3/4 cup chopped celery
1/2 cup (3 ounces) diced Dubuque 97% fat-free or any
    extra-lean ham
3/4 cup (3 ounces) Kraft shredded reduced-fat
    Cheddar cheese
2 hard-boiled eggs, diced
1/4 cup sweet pickle relish
1/2 cup Kraft fat-free Ranch dressing
2 tablespoons Kraft fat-free mayonnaise
1 teaspoon prepared mustard
1/4 teaspoon black pepper

In a large bowl, combine macaroni, peas, celery, ham, Cheddar cheese, eggs, and pickle relish. In a small bowl, combine Ranch dressing, mayonnaise, mustard, and black pepper. Add to macaroni mixture. Toss gently to combine. Refrigerate until ready to serve.

Hint: 1 3/4 cups uncooked macaroni usually make about 2 cups cooked.

Each serving equals:

HE: 1 2/3 Pr (1/3 limited), 1 Br, 1/4 Ve, 1/2 Sl, 7 OC
214 Calories, 5 gm Fa, 12 gm Pr, 30 gm Ca, 616 mg So, 2 Fi
DIABETIC: 2 St, 1 Mt

Fire-and-Ice Pasta Salad

I created this salad when I had leftover rotini pasta and cucumbers sitting around from other dishes I was testing. Am I ever glad I did! It has quickly become a "new family favorite."

○ Serves 4 (1 cup)

> 2 cups cooked rotini pasta, rinsed and drained
> 1 cup chopped fresh tomatoes
> 1 cup chopped cucumbers
> ⅓ cup (1½ ounces) Kraft shredded reduced-fat mozzarella cheese
> ¼ cup Kraft fat-free Ranch dressing
> 1 teaspoon Dijon mustard
> 1 tablespoon fresh parsley or 1 teaspoon dried parsley flakes

In a medium bowl, combine rotini pasta, tomatoes, cucumbers, and cheese. Add Ranch dressing, mustard, and parsley. Mix gently to combine. Cover and refrigerate until ready to serve.

Hint: 1½ cups uncooked rotini pasta usually make about 2 cups cooked.

Each serving equals:

HE: 1 Br, 1 Ve, ½ Pr, ¼ Sl, 5 OC

158 Calories, 2 gm Fa, 7 gm Pr, 28 gm Ca, 303 mg So, 2 Fi

DIABETIC: 1½ St, 1 Ve, ½ Mt

Oriental Pasta Salad

The delightful flavors of this salad are a tribute to the wonderful tastes we have adopted from China's cuisine into our everyday cooking. ● Serves 6 (full ⅔ cup)

> 3 cups cooked rotini pasta, rinsed and drained
> 1½ cups fresh pea pods
> ½ cup chopped red or green bell peppers
> ¼ cup sliced green onions
> ¼ cup (1 ounce) chopped dry-roasted peanuts
> 2 tablespoons reduced-sodium soy sauce
> 2 tablespoons lemon juice
> 3 tablespoons Kraft fat-free mayonnaise
> Sugar substitute to equal 1 tablespoon sugar
> 2 tablespoons Peter Pan reduced-fat creamy peanut butter

In a large bowl combine rotini pasta, pea pods, bell pepper, onions, and peanuts. In a medium bowl, combine soy sauce, lemon juice, mayonnaise, sugar substitute, and peanut butter. Mix well until smooth, using a wire whisk. Add to pasta mixture. Toss gently to combine. Cover and refrigerate until ready to serve. Toss again just before serving.

Hint: 2½ cups uncooked rotini pasta usually make about 3 cups cooked.

Each serving equals:

HE: 1 Br, ¾ Ve, ⅔ Fa, ½ Pr, 4 OC
195 Calories, 6 gm Fa, 7 gm Pr, 29 gm Ca, 99 mg So, 3 Fi
DIABETIC: 1½ St, 1 Ve, 1 Fa

Garden Pasta Salad

Haven't you always wished for a farmer's market, right at your own table? Full of texture, color, and taste, this salad will make your family rush to eat their vegetables. ☻ Serves 8 (1 cup)

> 3 cups cooked rotini pasta, rinsed and drained
> 1 cup chopped carrots
> 1 cup chopped celery
> 1 cup frozen peas, thawed
> ½ cup diced green bell pepper
> ½ cup chopped onion
> 1 cup chopped broccoli
> ⅛ teaspoon lemon pepper
> 1 cup Kraft fat-free French dressing

In a large bowl, combine rotini pasta, carrots, celery, peas, green pepper, onion, and broccoli. Add lemon pepper and French dressing. Mix well to combine. Cover and refrigerate for several hours.

Hint: 2½ cups uncooked rotini pasta usually make about 3 cups cooked.

Each serving equals:

HE: 1 Br, 1 Ve, ½ Sl

139 Calories, 1 gm Fa, 4 gm Pr, 29 gm Ca, 282 mg So, 3 Fi

DIABETIC: 2 Ve, 1 St

Sweet Salads

We have a delicious tradition in the Midwest (as do the Pennsylvania Dutch in the East) of serving sweet and fruity side dishes to accompany our hearty meals and satisfying suppers. Those with a base of flavored gelatin are sometimes called "molded" salads. These delectable concoctions combine healthy portions of fruit with a sprinkling of nuts, coconut, or marshmallows, and other flavors from yogurt and whipped topping to extracts and soft drinks. I like to say that I take something good—and good for you—and make it something special! What else do I love about my sweet Healthy Exchanges® salads? They look wonderful, they add color and sparkle to your table, and they're often tasty enough to qualify as dessert!

Blueberry Salad

The only things I left out of this "traditional" fruit salad are the fats and sugars. If you've never savored the combination of blueberries and pineapple, you've been missing something really special. ❍ Serves 8

2 (4-serving) packages Jell-O sugar-free raspberry gelatin
2 cups boiling water
1 cup (one 8-ounce can) crushed pineapple, packed in its
    own juice, drained (reserve liquid)
2 teaspoons lemon juice
3 cups fresh blueberries
1 cup chopped celery

In a large bowl, combine dry gelatin and the 2 cups of boiling water. Mix well to dissolve gelatin. Add enough water to reserved pineapple juice to make 1 cup liquid; add lemon juice to liquid. Blend liquid into gelatin mixture. Cool slightly. Stir in blueberries, pineapple, and celery. Pour into 8-by-8-inch glass dish. Refrigerate until set, about 4 hours. When serving, cut into 8 pieces.

Hint: Frozen blueberries (no sugar added), thawed and drained, can be used in place of fresh.

Each serving equals:

HE: ³/₄ Fr, ¹/₄ Ve, 8 OC
63 Calories, 0 gm Fa, 2 gm Pr, 14 gm Ca, 71 mg So, 2 Fi
DIABETIC: 1 Fr

Lime-Pear Salad

This was one of my mother's favorite salads, and one I remember eating with pleasure all through my childhood. Now that so many sugar-free and fat-free products are available, I don't have to give up one of the "comfort" foods of my youth. ☻ Serves 6

1 cup boiling water
2 cups (one 16-ounce can) pears, packed in their own juice,
  drained and chopped (reserve juice)
1 (4-serving) package Jell-O sugar-free lime gelatin
¾ cup fat-free cottage cheese

In a medium bowl, combine boiling water and reserved pear juice. Add dry gelatin. Mix well to dissolve gelatin. Refrigerate for about 15 minutes. Stir in cottage cheese. Whip with wire whisk until fluffy. Add pears. Mix gently to combine. Pour into 8-by-8-inch dish. Refrigerate until set, about 4 hours. When serving, cut into 6 pieces.

Each serving equals:

HE: ⅔ Fr, ¼ Pr, 5 OC

65 Calories, 0 gm Fa, 5 gm Pr, 12 gm Ca, 145 mg So, 1 Fi

DIABETIC: 1 Fr

Red Raspberry Salad

If you are a raspberry lover, then this is the salad for you. I know that in the Midwest we often serve salads that elsewhere would be considered desserts. This is a perfect example of what I mean. Enjoy—and save room for a Healthy Exchanges® pie!

● Serves 8

> 2 (4-serving) packages Jell-O sugar-free raspberry gelatin
> 2 cups boiling water
> 2¼ cups frozen red raspberries (no sugar added)
> 1½ cups unsweetened applesauce
> ¾ cup plain fat-free yogurt
> ⅓ cup Carnation nonfat dry milk powder
> Sugar substitute to equal 1 tablespoon sugar
> ½ cup Cool Whip Lite
> ¼ teaspoon vanilla extract
> 1 cup (2 ounces) miniature marshmallows

In a large bowl, combine dry gelatin with boiling water. Mix well to dissolve gelatin. Cool 5 minutes. Blend in raspberries and applesauce. Pour into 9-by-13-inch dish. Refrigerate until set, about 4 hours. In a small bowl, combine yogurt and dry milk powder. Blend in sugar substitute, Cool Whip Lite, and vanilla extract. Fold in marshmallows. Spread mixture evenly on top of set gelatin mixture. Refrigerate until ready to serve. When serving, cut into 8 pieces.

Each serving equals:

HE: ¾ Fr, ¼ SM, ¼ Sl, 9 OC

97 Calories, 1 gm Fa, 4 gm Pr, 19 gm Ca, 91 mg So, 1 Fi

DIABETIC: 1 Fr, ½ St

Refreshing Rhubarb Relish

Even if you think you don't like rhubarb—or if you've never tried it—this refreshing dish will win you over and change the way you look at this fruit that has so many fans in my part of the country.

● Serves 6

2 cups diced rhubarb
½ cup hot water
1 (4-serving) package Jell-O sugar-free raspberry,
*   strawberry, or lemon gelatin*
1 cup cold water
1 cup unpeeled apples, cored and chopped (2 small)
¼ cup raisins
⅓ cup (1½ ounces) chopped walnuts

In a medium saucepan, cook rhubarb in hot water until soft, about 10 minutes. Dissolve dry gelatin in hot rhubarb sauce. Add cold water and stir well. Blend in apples, raisins, and walnuts. Mix gently to combine. Pour into 8-by-8-inch dish. Refrigerate until set, about 4 hours. When serving, cut into 6 pieces.

Hints: 1. Good served with 1 teaspoon fat-free mayonnaise on top. If used, count optional calories accordingly.
2. To plump up raisins without "cooking," place in glass measuring cup and microwave on HIGH for 15 seconds.

Each serving equals:

HE: ⅔ Fr, ⅔ Ve, ½ Fa, ¼ Pr, 5 OC

94 Calories, 4 gm Fa, 3 gm Pr, 12 gm Ca, 39 mg So, 2 Fi

DIABETIC: 1 Fr, 1 Fa

Holiday Salad

This festive creation is as attractive as any gift under the Christmas tree. The best part: All who partake of this jewel of a salad will thank you for a delicious present. ● Serves 8

1 (4-serving) package Jell-O sugar-free lime gelatin
3 cups boiling water ☆
1 (8-ounce) package Philadelphia fat-free cream cheese
1 cup (one 8-ounce can) crushed pineapple, packed in its
    own juice, drained
Sugar substitute to equal 2 teaspoons sugar
½ teaspoon vanilla extract
¼ cup (1 ounce) chopped pecans
1 (4-serving) package Jell-O sugar-free strawberry gelatin

In a medium bowl, combine dry lime gelatin and 1½ cups boiling water. Mix well to dissolve gelatin. Pour mixture into an 8-by-8-inch dish. Refrigerate until set, about 2 hours. In a medium bowl, stir cream cheese with a spoon until soft. Add drained pineapple, sugar substitute, vanilla extract, and pecans. Mix well to combine. Spread mixture over set lime gelatin. Refrigerate for about 15 minutes. Meanwhile, in a medium bowl, combine dry strawberry gelatin and remaining 1½ cups boiling water. Mix well to dissolve gelatin. Refrigerate gelatin mixture for about 15 minutes. Pour cooled strawberry gelatin evenly over cream cheese layer. Refrigerate for at least 2 hours. When serving, cut into 8 pieces.

Each serving equals:

HE: ½ Pr, ½ Fa, ¼ Fr, 8 OC
72 Calories, 2 gm Fa, 6 gm Pr, 7 gm Ca, 225 mg So, 0 Fi
DIABETIC: ½ Fr, ½ Mt

Lemon-Lime Applesauce Salad

I based this salad on that old mainstay that's served at just about any church supper in America—but my version is not only good, it's good for you. The unsweetened applesauce is part of the liquid to dissolve the gelatin and adds delicious flavor to an already scrumptious salad. ☻ Serves 8

> 3 cups unsweetened applesauce
> 2 (4-serving) packages Jell-O sugar-free lemon gelatin
> 1 cup diet lemon-lime soda
> 3/4 cup plain fat-free yogurt
> 1/3 cup Carnation nonfat dry milk powder
> 1 cup Cool Whip Lite

In a medium saucepan, heat applesauce to boiling. Remove from heat. Stir in dry gelatin. Mix well to dissolve gelatin. Add lemon-lime soda. Refrigerate for 30 minutes. In a large bowl, combine yogurt and dry milk powder. Stir in Cool Whip Lite. Gently fold yogurt mixture into gelatin mixture. Pour into 8-by-8-inch dish. Refrigerate for at least 4 hours. To serve, cut into 8 pieces.

Each serving equals:

HE: 3/4 Fr, 1/4 SM, 1/4 Sl, 4 OC

78 Calories, 1 gm Fa, 3 gm Pr, 15 gm Ca, 78 mg So, 1 Fi

DIABETIC: 1 Fr

Strawberry Dessert Salad

I love strawberries in any way, shape, or form. If you do, too, then this all-year-round salad will make your "Top Ten" list of salads for every occasion. ●   Serves 6

¾ cup plain fat-free yogurt
⅓ cup Carnation nonfat dry milk powder
½ cup Cool Whip Lite
Sugar substitute to equal 1 tablespoon sugar
4 cups frozen strawberries, thawed and sliced (no sugar added)
1 cup (one 8-ounce can) crushed pineapple, packed in its own juice, drained
1 cup (2 ounces) miniature marshmallows

In a medium bowl, combine yogurt and dry milk powder. Blend in Cool Whip Lite and sugar substitute. Add strawberries, pineapple, and marshmallows. Mix gently to combine. Spoon into 6 dessert dishes. Refrigerate for at least 2 hours.

Each serving equals:

HE: 1 Fr, ⅓ SM, ¼ Sl, 8 OC
126 Calories, 1 gm Fa, 4 gm Pr, 26 gm Ca, 51 mg So, 2 Fi
DIABETIC: 1 Fr, ½ SM

Strawberry Rice Salad

If you think strawberry flavor and rice don't sound as though they go together, you'll be deliciously surprised when you try this attractive dish. ●   Serves 4 (1 cup)

> 1 (4-serving) package Jell-O sugar-free strawberry gelatin
> ½ cup boiling water
> 2 cups (two 8-ounce cans) crushed pineapple, packed in its own juice, undrained
> 2 cups cooked rice
> 1 cup Cool Whip Lite
> ¾ cup plain fat-free yogurt
> ½ teaspoon vanilla extract

In a medium bowl, combine dry gelatin and boiling water. Mix well to dissolve gelatin. Blend in pineapple with juice. Stir in rice. Let partially set (about 1 hour). Stir in Cool Whip Lite, yogurt, and vanilla extract. Refrigerate for at least 1 hour.

Hint: 1⅓ cups uncooked rice usually make about 2 cups cooked.

Each serving equals:

HE: 1 Br, 1 Fr, ¼ SM, 1 Sl

207 Calories, 2 gm Fa, 6 gm Pr, 42 gm Ca, 93 mg So, 2 Fi

DIABETIC: 2 St, 1 Fr

Mandarin Orange Salad

Here's an easy way to bring sunshine into your life—and onto your table—any time of the year. The combination of mandarin oranges and pineapple is truly a culinary treat—and healthy, too!

○ Serves 8

1 (4-serving) package Jell-O sugar-free orange gelatin
1 cup boiling water
½ cup cold water
1 cup (one 8-ounce can) crushed pineapple, packed in its
    own juice, undrained
1 cup (one 11-ounce can) mandarin oranges, rinsed and
    drained
¾ cup plain fat-free yogurt
⅓ cup Carnation nonfat dry milk powder
1 cup Cool Whip Lite

In a large bowl, combine dry gelatin and boiling water. Stir in cold water and pineapple with juice. Blend in oranges. Refrigerate for 30 minutes. In a medium bowl, combine yogurt and dry milk powder. Blend in Cool Whip Lite. Gently fold yogurt mixture into gelatin mixture. Pour into 8-by-8-inch dish. Refrigerate for at least 4 hours. When serving, cut into 8 pieces.

Each serving equals:

HE: ½ Fr, ¼ SM, ¼ Sl
73 Calories, 1 gm Fa, 3 gm Pr, 13 gm Ca, 62 mg So, 1 Fi
DIABETIC: 1 Fr

Glorified Rice

One taste of this rice salad and you will know why it's called glorified! The almond extract takes the bitter taste away from the yogurt. ☺ Serves 4 (1 cup)

2 cups cooked rice

2 cups (one 16-ounce can) fruit cocktail, packed in its own juice, drained

½ cup (1 ounce) miniature marshmallows

¾ cup plain fat-free yogurt

⅓ cup Carnation nonfat dry milk powder

¾ cup Cool Whip Lite

Sugar substitute to equal 2 tablespoons sugar

1 teaspoon almond extract

In a medium bowl, combine rice, fruit cocktail, and marshmallows. In a small bowl, combine yogurt and dry milk powder. Stir in Cool Whip Lite, sugar substitute, and almond extract. Blend into rice mixture. Refrigerate for at least 2 hours.

Hint: 1⅓ cups uncooked rice usually make about 2 cups cooked.

Each serving equals:

HE: 1 Br, 1 Fr, ½ SM, ½ Sl

216 Calories, 2 gm Fa, 6 gm Pr, 44 gm Ca, 78 mg So, 1 Fi

DIABETIC: 2 St, 1 Fr

Mandarin–Cottage Cheese Salad

This old-time favorite was served at just about every family potluck in the '60's. Now I've brought it up to date with the same wonderful flavor combination—but much less sugar and fat.

⌾ Serves 8 (³/₄ cup)

³/₄ cup plain fat-free yogurt
²/₃ cup Carnation nonfat dry milk powder
1 teaspoon coconut extract
2 cups fat-free cottage cheese
1 cup (one 8-ounce can) crushed pineapple, packed in its
  own juice, drained
1 cup (one 11-ounce can) mandarin oranges, rinsed and
  drained
1 cup Cool Whip Lite
1 (4-serving) package Jell-O sugar-free orange gelatin

In a large bowl combine yogurt and dry milk powder. Stir in coconut extract and cottage cheese. Add pineapple, mandarin oranges, and Cool Whip Lite. Sprinkle dry gelatin over top. Gently stir to combine. Cover and refrigerate for 4 to 6 hours.

Each serving equals:
HE: ½ Pr, ½ Fr, ¼ SM, ¼ Sl
103 Calories, 1 gm Fa, 8 gm Pr, 16 gm Ca, 183 mg So, 0 Fi
DIABETIC: 1 Mt, ½ Fr, ½ Fa

Pink Champagne Salad

The strawberries are the star of this beautiful salad. It's as close as you will get to heaven with an earthly taste treat.

◐ Serves 6 (²/₃ cup)

³/₄ cup plain fat-free yogurt
¹/₃ cup Carnation nonfat dry milk powder
Sugar substitute to equal 2 tablespoons sugar
1 teaspoon vanilla extract
1 cup Cool Whip Lite
2–3 drops red food coloring
1 cup (one 8-ounce can) crushed pineapple, packed in its
*   own juice, undrained*
1 (4-serving) package sugar-free instant vanilla pudding mix
2 cups coarsely chopped fresh strawberries
¹/₂ cup (1 ounce) miniature marshmallows

In a large bowl combine yogurt and dry milk powder. Add sugar substitute, vanilla extract, Cool Whip Lite, and red food coloring. Mix gently to combine. Add pineapple with juice and dry pudding mix. Mix well using a wire whisk. Fold in strawberries and marshmallows. Cover and refrigerate for at least 30 minutes.

Each serving equals:

HE: ²/₃ Fr, ¹/₃ SM, ¹/₂ Sl, 8 OC

123 Calories, 1 gm Fa, 3 gm Pr, 25 gm Ca, 261 mg So, 1 Fi

DIABETIC: 1 Fr, ¹/₂ St

Lemon Fluff Salad

So easy, yet so elegant. The delicate flavor of the lemon plays wonderfully against the fruit cocktail. ●   Serves 6 (⅔ cup)

> 1 (4-serving) package Jell-O sugar-free instant vanilla
>   pudding mix
> 1 (4-serving) package Jell-O sugar-free lemon gelatin
> ⅔ cup Carnation nonfat dry milk powder
> 1¼ cups water
> 2 cups (one 16-ounce can) fruit cocktail, packed in fruit
>   juice, drained (reserve liquid)
> ¾ cup Cool Whip Lite
> ½ cup (1 ounce) miniature marshmallows

In a medium bowl, combine dry pudding mix, dry gelatin, and dry milk powder. Add water and reserved fruit cocktail liquid to dry pudding mixture. Mix well using a wire whisk. Blend in Cool Whip Lite, fruit cocktail, and miniature marshmallows. Cover and refrigerate for at least 30 minutes.

Each serving equals:

HE: ⅔ Fr, ⅓ SM, ½ Sl, 6 OC

120 Calories, 1 gm Fa, 4 gm Pr, 24 gm Ca, 296 mg So, 0 Fi

DIABETIC: 1 Fr, ½ St

Strawberry–Banana Split Salad

The dictionary defines strawberries as 1) a small, juicy, red, edible fruit and 2) the low plant of the rose family it grows on. I define strawberries as the most wonderful food on earth! If you share my love of strawberries, I think you will enjoy this salad as much as I do. ❍ Serves 6 (¾ cup)

> 1 (4-serving) package Jell-O sugar-free instant vanilla
>   pudding mix
> ⅔ cup Carnation nonfat dry milk powder
> 1 cup water
> 1 cup (one 8-ounce can) pineapple tidbits, packed in their
>   own juice, drained (reserve liquid)
> ½ cup Cool Whip Lite
> 1 cup diced banana (1 medium)
> 2 cups fresh strawberries, sliced
> 2 tablespoons (½ ounce) chopped pecans
> 2 tablespoons (½ ounce) mini chocolate chips

In a large bowl combine dry pudding mix and dry milk powder. Add water and drained pineapple juice. Mix well using a wire whisk. Blend in Cool Whip Lite. Add pineapple tidbits, diced banana, sliced strawberries, chopped pecans, and mini chocolate chips. Mix gently to combine. Cover and refrigerate until ready to serve.

Hints: 1. If you can't find pineapple tidbits, use pineapple chunks and chop coarsely.
2. To prevent banana from turning brown, mix diced banana with 1 teaspoon lemon juice.

Each serving equals:

HE: ⅓ SM, ⅓ Fr, ⅓ Fa, ½ Sl
134 Calories, 3 gm Fa, 3 gm Pr, 25 gm Ca, 136 mg So, 2 Fi
DIABETIC: 2 Fr

Five-Cup Salad

I can still remember the first time my sister Mary served the original of this salad at a family potluck more than thirty-five years ago. I fell in love with this salad then and enjoy it just as much in its "scaled-down" version now. The name comes from the original recipe, which included one cup each of five ingredients mixed together to create what some families call "Ambrosia." See if you don't agree it tastes as good as "food for the gods." ❂ Serves 4 (2/3 cup)

> 1 cup (one 11-ounce can) mandarin oranges, rinsed and
>   drained
> 1 cup (one 8-ounce can) pineapple chunks, packed in their
>   own juice, drained
> 2 tablespoons flaked coconut
> 1/2 cup (1 ounce) miniature marshmallows
> 3/4 cup plain fat-free yogurt
> Sugar substitute to equal 4 teaspoons sugar
> 1 teaspoon coconut extract

In a medium bowl, combine orange sections, pineapple chunks, coconut, and marshmallows. In a small bowl, combine yogurt, sugar substitute, and coconut extract. Add to orange mixture. Mix gently to combine. Cover and refrigerate for at least 2 hours.

Each serving equals:

HE: 1 Fr, 1/4 SM, 1/4 Sl, 2 OC

128 Calories, 1 gm Fa, 3 gm Pr, 27 gm Ca, 49 mg So, 1 Fi

DIABETIC: 2 Fr

Vegetables

O kay, so we've been told that one of the best ways to assure good health for a lifetime is to eat at least five servings of fruits and vegetables each day, to get the fiber and nutrients we need. But if the same old vegetables have been appearing night after night on your table, maybe some delicious Healthy Exchanges® recipes will get your family enthusiastic about eating their veggies again. Here you'll find easy ways to add flavor, color, and texture to your vegetables and see how new combinations of flavors can change how you look at this essential food group.

Green Beans

and Stuffing Supreme

Yes, this is based on that great American mainstay of the '50s. If you loved it then, enjoy it now but without any guilt. It's perfect for any family celebration, makes an excellent company dish, and lets you remember the good old days. ☻ Serves 4

1 (10³/₄-ounce) can Campbell's Healthy Request Cream of
    Mushroom Soup
1 tablespoon flour
³/₄ cup plain fat-free yogurt
1 tablespoon dried onion flakes
¹/₄ teaspoon salt
¹/₈ teaspoon black pepper
4 cups frozen green beans, cooked and drained
2 cups (one 16-ounce can) Campbell's Healthy Request
    Chicken Broth
2 cups (3 ounces) purchased herb-seasoned bread cubes

Preheat oven to 350 degrees. In a saucepan, combine mushroom soup, flour, yogurt, onion flakes, salt, and black pepper. Stir in green beans. Spray an 8-by-8-inch baking dish with butter-flavored cooking spray. Pour mixture into dish. In a medium bowl, combine chicken broth and dry stuffing mix. Stir until blended and soft. Evenly sprinkle stuffing mixture on top of bean mixture. Cover. Bake 25 minutes; uncover and bake an additional 5 minutes.

Hint: Brownberry bread cubes taste great in this recipe.

Each serving equals:
    HE: 2 Ve, 1 Br, ¹/₄ SM, ¹/₂ Sl, 17 OC
    205 Calories, 3 gm Fa, 9 gm Pr, 36 gm Ca, 741 mg So, 2 Fi
    DIABETIC: 2 Ve, 2 St

Green Bean Melody

Here's another creamy, tangy way to eat your green beans. A lot of people tell me that green beans are one of the only vegetables they like to eat, so you'll discover it's smart to have several delicious, different ways to prepare them. ● Serves 6 (1 cup)

2 cups cooked rotini pasta, rinsed and drained

3 cups frozen green beans, cooked and drained

1 cup (one 4-ounce can) canned sliced mushrooms, drained

1 (10¾-ounce) can Campbell's Healthy Request Cream of Mushroom Soup

½ teaspoon lemon pepper

½ teaspoon dried basil

1 tablespoon + 1 teaspoon reduced-calorie margarine

½ cup (1½ ounces) grated Kraft House Italian or Parmesan cheese

In a large saucepan, combine rotini pasta and green beans. Stir in mushrooms. Add mushroom soup, lemon pepper, and basil. Mix well. Add margarine and House Italian cheese. Continue cooking until heated through.

Hint: 1½ cups uncooked rotini pasta usually make about 2 cups cooked.

Each serving equals:

HE: 1⅓ Ve, ⅔ Br, ⅓ Fa, ⅓ Pr, ¼ Sl, 8 OC

153 Calories, 4 gm Fa, 7 gm Pr, 22 gm Ca, 741 mg So, 1 Fi

DIABETIC: 1 Ve, 1 St, ½ Mt

Perky Green Beans

Here's my version of the classic dish fancy restaurants call Green Beans Amandine. Whatever you call it, it's a satisfying taste treat that will perk up anybody's taste buds. Try it and see!

○ Serves 4 (³/₄ cup)

3 cups fresh or frozen green beans
1 tablespoon + 1 teaspoon reduced-calorie margarine
¼ cup (1 ounce) slivered almonds
2 teaspoons lemon juice
⅛ teaspoon lemon pepper

In a medium saucepan, cook beans in water until tender, about 15 minutes. Drain. Transfer beans to serving dish and keep warm. Meanwhile, in a small skillet, melt margarine. Stir in almonds, lemon juice, and lemon pepper. Cook over medium heat until heated through, about 3 to 4 minutes. Pour mixture over beans. Toss gently to combine. Serve at once.

Each serving equals:

HE: 1½ Ve, 1 Fa, ¼ Pr
84 Calories, 5 gm Fa, 3 gm Pr, 7 gm Ca, 23 mg So, 1 Fi
DIABETIC: 1½ Ve, 1 Fa

Zesty Broccoli

The zest comes when you add mustard and horseradish to this creamy broccoli dish. Even if you turn your nose up at the combination—or you're not a fan of broccoli—please give this delectable dish a try. I think you'll be glad you did.

● Serves 4 (¾ cup)

> 1½ cups (one 12-fluid-ounce can) Carnation evaporated skim milk
> 3 tablespoons flour
> ¼ teaspoon lemon pepper
> 1 teaspoon prepared mustard
> 1 teaspoon prepared horseradish
> 3 cups (one 16-ounce bag) frozen cut broccoli, cooked and drained

In a covered jar, combine evaporated skim milk, flour, and lemon pepper. Shake well. Pour into a medium saucepan sprayed with butter-flavored cooking spray. Cook over medium heat, stirring constantly until mixture thickens. Stir in mustard and horseradish. Add broccoli and stir until blended. Serve at once.

Each serving equals:

HE: 1½ Ve, ¾ SM, ¼ Br

116 Calories, 0 gm Fa, 10 gm Pr, 19 gm Ca, 145 mg So, 4 Fi

DIABETIC: 1½ Ve, 1 SM

Cabbage-Carrot Curry

This savory cabbage dish becomes extra-special with the addition of one winning ingredient—just a bit of curry powder. If you've never tried it, you may be surprised by its wonderful flavor and color. ● Serves 4 (1 cup)

4 cups coarsely chopped cabbage

1 cup shredded carrots

½ teaspoon curry powder

¼ teaspoon mustard seed

⅛ teaspoon black pepper

⅔ cup Carnation nonfat dry milk powder

½ cup water

1 tablespoon + 1 teaspoon reduced-calorie margarine

In a large skillet sprayed with butter-flavored cooking spray, combine cabbage, carrots, curry powder, mustard seed, and black pepper. In a small bowl, combine dry milk powder and water. Combine milk and margarine with cabbage mixture. Cover. Cook over medium heat until cabbage is tender and liquid is absorbed, about 6 minutes.

Each serving equals:

HE: 2½ Ve, ½ Fa, ½ SM

79 Calories, 1 gm Fa, 5 gm Pr, 12 gm Ca, 100 mg So, 2 Fi

DIABETIC: 1 Ve, ½ SM

Carrots au Gratin

I give this carrot recipe ten stars! You will, too, once you taste its cheesy-crunchy goodness. ☻   Serves 6

4 cups sliced carrots

3 cups water

¼ cup chopped onion

¼ cup chopped green bell pepper

1 cup (2 ounces) Ritz reduced-fat crackers, crushed

⅛ teaspoon lemon pepper

1 tablespoon + 1 teaspoon reduced-calorie margarine,
  melted

¾ cup (3 ounces) Kraft shredded reduced-fat Cheddar
  cheese

Preheat oven to 425 degrees. In a large saucepan, cook carrots in water until tender but still crisp, about 10 minutes. Drain. In a skillet sprayed with butter-flavored cooking spray, sauté onion and green pepper until tender, about 5 minutes. In a large bowl, combine crackers, onion, green pepper, and lemon pepper. Spray an 8-by-8-inch baking dish with butter-flavored cooking spray. Alternate 2 layers of carrots and crumb mixture, ending with crumbs. Pour melted margarine over top and sprinkle with cheese. Bake 15 to 20 minutes or until cheese melts.

Each serving equals:

HE: 1½ Ve, ⅔ Pr, ⅓ Fa, ⅓ Br, ¼ Sl

125 Calories, 5 gm Fa, 5 gm Pr, 14 gm Ca, 227 mg So, 3 Fi

DIABETIC: 1 Ve, ½ Mt, ½ Fa, ½ St

Cheddar Cheese-Carrot Quiche

This easy dish is so satisfying, you won't even miss the crust. It's a great luncheon dish. Those high-in-beta-carotene carrots deliver lots of flavor and nourishment in just one piece. ☻ Serves 4

1 cup shredded carrots
1 cup water ☆
⅓ cup Carnation nonfat dry milk powder
2 eggs or equivalent in egg substitute
2 tablespoons chopped green or white onion
½ teaspoon lemon pepper
¼ teaspoon ginger
1 teaspoon dried parsley flakes
¾ cup (3 ounces) Kraft shredded reduced-fat Cheddar
    cheese

Preheat oven to 350 degrees. In a medium saucepan, cook carrots in ½ cup of water. Bring mixture to a boil. Cover and remove from heat. Let stand 5 minutes; then drain. In a medium bowl, combine dry milk powder, remaining ½ cup water, eggs, onion, lemon pepper, ginger, and parsley flakes. Mix well to combine. Stir in drained carrots and Cheddar cheese. To bake, pour 2 cups hot water into 8-by-8-inch baking dish. Spray four 1-cup custard cups with butter-flavored cooking spray. Pour carrot mixture evenly into custard cups and place filled cups in baking dish with water. Bake 35 to 40 minutes or until knife inserted in center comes out clean.

Each serving equals:

HE: 1½ Pr (½ limited), ½ Ve, ¼ SM
123 Calories, 5 gm Fa, 12 gm Pr, 7 gm Ca, 243 mg So, 1 Fi
DIABETIC: 1½ Mt, 1 Ve

Au Gratin Cabbage

This cabbage recipe smells like perfume for the kitchen, with its blend of cheeses baked crusty and bubbling. Just wait until you taste it! ❷   Serves 6

4 cups water
7½ cups chopped cabbage
1 (10¾-ounce) can Campbell's Healthy Request Cream of
   Mushroom Soup
1 scant cup (3¾ ounces) Kraft shredded reduced-fat
   Cheddar cheese
⅛ teaspoon black pepper
6 tablespoons (1½ ounces) dried bread crumbs
¼ cup (¾ ounce) grated Kraft House Italian or Parmesan
   cheese
1 teaspoon dried parsley flakes

Preheat oven to 350 degrees. In a large saucepan, bring water to a boil. Add cabbage and cook until tender, about 6 minutes. Drain. Combine mushroom soup, Cheddar cheese, and black pepper in a saucepan. Heat, stirring, until cheese melts. Combine with cabbage. Place cabbage mixture in an 8-by-8-inch baking dish coated with butter-flavored cooking spray. Toss bread crumbs with House Italian cheese and parsley flakes. Sprinkle on top of cabbage. Lightly spray top of casserole with butter-flavored cooking spray. Bake 15 minutes or until thoroughly heated.

Each serving equals:

HE: 2½ Ve, 1 Pr, ⅓ Br, ¼ Sl, 13 OC
112 Calories, 4 gm Fa, 8 gm Pr, 11 gm Ca, 425 mg So, 2 Fi
DIABETIC: 2 Ve, 1 Mt, ½ St

Corn-Zucchini Bake

I have to admit that the only reason I created this recipe was that a neighbor gave me her excess zucchini from her garden. (If you grow zucchini, you know how hard it can be to find enough ways to use up your abundant harvest!) After just one bite of this, I became a zucchini fan for life. ● Serves 4

2 cups sliced zucchini
1 cup water
½ cup chopped onion
2 eggs, beaten, or equivalent in
    egg substitute
2 cups frozen whole-kernel corn,
    thawed
Two ¾-ounce slices Weight
    Watchers reduced-fat Swiss
    cheese, shredded

⅓ cup (1 ½ ounces) Kraft
    shredded reduced-fat Cheddar
    cheese
3 tablespoons (¾ ounce) dry
    bread crumbs
¼ cup (¾ ounce) grated Kraft
    House Italian or Parmesan
    cheese
1 teaspoon dried parsley flakes

Preheat oven to 350 degrees. In a covered medium saucepan, cook zucchini in water until tender, about 15 to 20 minutes. Drain and mash zucchini with fork. In a skillet sprayed with butter-flavored cooking spray, sauté onions until tender. Add mashed zucchini, eggs, corn, and cheese. Mix well to combine. Pour into an 8-by-8-inch baking dish sprayed with butter-flavored cooking spray. In a small bowl, combine bread crumbs, House Italian cheese, and parsley flakes. Sprinkle on top of zucchini mixture. Lightly spray with butter-flavored cooking spray. Bake 35 to 40 minutes or until knife inserted in center comes out clean. Let stand 5 to 10 minutes before serving.

Each serving equals:

　HE: 1¾ Pr (½ limited), 1¼ Ve, 1¼ Br
　236 Calories, 9 gm Fa, 15 gm Pr, 24 gm Ca, 437 mg So, 2 Fi
　DIABETIC: 2 Mt, 1 Ve, 1 St

Tomatoes with Mozzarella

You tell me—is this a vegetable dish or a salad? Whatever you decide, I'm sure "wonderful" will be part of your description.

● Serves 4 (full ½ cup)

2 cups diced fresh tomatoes
⅓ cup (1½ ounces) Kraft shredded reduced-fat mozzarella cheese
3 tablespoons Kraft fat-free Italian dressing
2 teaspoons dried basil

In a medium bowl, combine tomatoes, cheese, Italian dressing, and basil. Mix gently to combine. Cover and refrigerate for at least 1 hour.

Each serving equals:
HE: 1 Ve, ½ Pr, 3 OC
48 Calories, 2 gm Fa, 4 gm Pr, 4 gm Ca, 186 mg So, 1 Fi
DIABETIC: ½ Ve

Fried Tomatoes with Mushroom Sauce

This combination of fresh tomatoes, basil, and mushroom soup is as close to perfection as a vegetable dish may ever come.

- Serves 6 (scant ½ cup)

6 tablespoons flour

¼ teaspoon lemon pepper

4 fresh medium red tomatoes, sliced

1 tablespoon + 1 teaspoon reduced-calorie margarine

1 (10¾-ounce) can Campbell's Healthy Request Cream of Mushroom Soup

1 tablespoon fresh basil, chopped, or 1 teaspoon dried basil

In a saucer, combine flour and lemon pepper. Dip tomato slices in flour mixture. Melt margarine in a large skillet. Place tomato slices in skillet. Cook tomatoes over low heat until lightly browned on both sides. Remove to heated platter. Stir mushroom soup and basil into skillet. Heat. Pour sauce evenly over tomatoes. Serve at once.

Each serving equals:

HE: ⅔ Ve, ⅓ Br, ⅓ Fa, ¼ Sl, 8 OC

81 Calories, 2 gm Fa, 2 gm Pr, 14 gm Ca, 229 mg So, 1 Fi

DIABETIC: 1 Ve, ½ St, ½ Fa

Tomato Pie

I served this at a town potluck and had everyone who sampled it begging me for the recipe. It's filling enough to satisfy even a truck-drivin' man like Cliff! ☻   Serves 8

1 Pillsbury refrigerated unbaked 9-inch pie crust
4 fresh medium red tomatoes, peeled and sliced
½ cup Kraft fat-free mayonnaise
2 teaspoons Worcestershire sauce
2 teaspoons Sprinkle Sweet or Sugar Twin
1½ cups (6 ounces) Kraft shredded reduced-fat Cheddar
   cheese
1 tablespoon dried parsley flakes

Preheat oven to 450 degrees. Place pie crust in 9-inch pie plate. Flute edges. Bake until crust is light brown, but *not* done, about 6 minutes. Remove from oven. Lower heat to 350 degrees. Place a layer of sliced tomatoes in pie crust. In a small bowl, combine mayonnaise, Worcestershire sauce, Sprinkle Sweet, and Cheddar cheese. Spread ⅓ of mixture over tomatoes, cover with more tomatoes, and repeat until 3 layers of each are in pie crust. Top with parsley flakes. Bake 30 minutes. Let cool 2 to 3 minutes before cutting.

Each serving equals:
   HE: 1 Pr, ½ Br, ½ Ve, ½ Sl, 18 OC
   195 Calories, 10 gm Fa, 7 gm Pr, 19 gm Ca, 445 mg So, 2 Fi
   DIABETIC: 1 Mt, 1 St, 1 Fa, ½ Ve

Tomato-Potato-Zucchini Pie

Once you come to terms with the idea that the crust is made from shredded potatoes instead of the traditional pastry, I think you will find this unusual pie a true summer delight. ☻ Serves 6

3 cups (10 ounces) shredded frozen potatoes, slightly thawed
1 cup diced onion ☆
1 egg, beaten, or equivalent in egg substitute
3 tablespoons flour
½ teaspoon dried parsley flakes
8 (¾-ounce) slices Weight Watchers reduced-fat Swiss
*   cheese, shredded ☆*
2 cups thinly sliced zucchini
2 cups sliced fresh tomatoes
1 teaspoon Italian seasoning
¼ teaspoon lemon pepper

Preheat oven to 350 degrees. In a medium bowl, combine shredded potatoes, ½ cup onion, egg, flour, and parsley flakes. Mix well to combine. Pat mixture into a 9-inch pie plate sprayed with olive-flavored cooking spray. Bake 30 minutes or until crust is lightly browned. Layer ¾ cup Swiss cheese in crust. Layer zucchini, tomato slices, and remaining ½ cup onion. Sprinkle Italian seasoning and lemon pepper over onions. Evenly sprinkle remaining ¾ cup Swiss cheese on top. Bake 40 to 45 minutes or until vegetables are tender.

Hint: Mr. Dell's shredded potatoes are a good choice for this recipe or raw shredded potatoes can be used in place of frozen ones.

Each serving equals:

HE: 1½ Pr, 1½ Ve, ½ Br
203 Calories, 8 gm Fa, 10 gm Pr, 23 gm Ca, 463 mg So, 3 Fi
DIABETIC: 1 Mt, 1 Ve, 1 St, 1 Fa

Scalloped Tomatoes

I'm a tomato fan—can you tell that by now? If you aren't now, this easy dish may convert you! ☻ Serves 4

3/4 cup chopped onion
1/4 cup chopped green bell pepper
3 cups (one 28-ounce can) coarsely chopped canned
*   tomatoes, with juice*
1 tablespoon prepared mustard
1 tablespoon Brown Sugar Twin
3/4 cup (3 ounces) dry bread crumbs
1 teaspoon taco seasoning mix
3/4 cup (3 ounces) Kraft shredded reduced-fat
*   Cheddar cheese*

Preheat oven to 350 degrees. In a large skillet sprayed with butter-flavored cooking spray, sauté onion and green pepper until tender. Add tomatoes with juice. Stir in mustard and Brown Sugar Twin. Add bread crumbs, taco seasoning, and Cheddar cheese. Mix well. Pour into 8-by-8-inch baking dish sprayed with butter-flavored cooking spray. Bake 30 to 35 minutes.

Each serving equals:

HE: 2 Ve, 1 Pr, 1 Br, 1 OC
196 Calories, 5 gm Fa, 11 gm Pr, 27 gm Ca, 693 mg So, 3 Fi
DIABETIC: 2 Ve, 1 Mt, 1 St

Cheesy Vegetable Sauté

This dish looks so attractive and tastes so good, your family will never complain about eating their "daily five" servings. Bring on the veggies! ❍ Serves 4

1 tablespoon + 1 teaspoon reduced-calorie margarine
1 cup green bell pepper strips
1 cup red onion, cut into rings
1 teaspoon minced garlic
1/2 teaspoon dried basil
2 cups peeled and chopped fresh tomatoes
3/4 cup (3 ounces) Kraft shredded reduced-fat
   mozzarella cheese

In a large skillet, melt margarine. Add peppers, onion, garlic, and basil. Sauté until vegetables are crisp-tender, about 5 minutes. Stir in tomatoes. Sprinkle mozzarella cheese over top. Cover and continue cooking until cheese is melted, about 3 minutes. Serve immediately.

Each serving equals:

HE: 1 1/2 Ve, 1 Pr, 1/2 Fa
95 Calories, 4 gm Fa, 7 gm Pr, 7 gm Ca, 243 mg So, 2 Fi
DIABETIC: 1 Ve, 1 Mt, 1/2 Fa

Italian Potato-Vegetable Bake

Ready in just 30 minutes, this delicious vegetable dish looks like you fussed for hours. My son Tommy said, "Yes, yes, yes" to this satisfying veggie casserole—and I know you will, too!

○ Serves 4

3 cups (15 ounces) raw potatoes, thickly sliced
1 (16-ounce) package frozen carrot, broccoli, and cauliflower blend vegetables
3 cups water
1/2 cup (one 2.5-ounce jar) canned sliced mushrooms, drained

2 teaspoons Italian seasoning
1/8 teaspoon black pepper
1 3/4 cups (one 15-ounce can) Hunt's Chunky Tomato Sauce
3/4 cup (3 ounces) Kraft shredded reduced-fat mozzarella cheese

Preheat oven to 350 degrees. In a medium saucepan, cook potatoes and vegetable blend in water until potatoes are almost tender, about 20 minutes. Drain. Spray 8-by-8-inch baking dish with butter-flavored cooking spray. In a medium bowl, combine potato-and-vegetable mixture with mushrooms, Italian seasoning, and black pepper. Pour into baking dish. Pour tomato sauce evenly over top. Sprinkle mozzarella cheese over tomato sauce. Bake 30 minutes.

Hints: 1. 1 cup frozen carrots, 1 cup frozen cauliflower, and 1 cup frozen broccoli can be used instead of blended vegetables.
2. A scant 1 cup (4 ounces) diced cooked chicken breast can be added to make this a main-dish treat.

Each serving equals:
HE: 3 1/2 Ve, 1 Pr, 3/4 Br
211 Calories, 5 gm Fa, 11 gm Pr, 31 gm Ca, 937 mg So, 5 Fi
DIABETIC: 3 Ve, 1 St, 1 Mt

Creamy Corn Scallop

Here's a healthy and delicious version of a corn pudding that I think you'll want to prepare again and again. It's so easy—and so good. ❂ Serves 6

1 (10¾-ounce) can Campbell's Healthy Request Cream of
  Mushroom Soup
2 tablespoons dried onion flakes
½ teaspoon dry mustard or 1 teaspoon prepared mustard
⅛ teaspoon black pepper
2 teaspoons Sprinkle Sweet or Sugar Twin
2 cups (one 16-ounce can) canned whole-kernel corn, rinsed
  and drained
1 cup (2 ounces) crushed Ritz reduced-fat crackers

Preheat oven to 350 degrees. In a medium bowl, combine mushroom soup, onion flakes, mustard, black pepper, and Sprinkle Sweet. Mix in corn and cracker crumbs. Pour into an 8-by-8-inch baking dish sprayed with butter-flavored cooking spray. Bake 25 minutes.

Each serving equals:

HE: 1 Br, ½ Sl, 8 OC
121 Calories, 3 gm Fa, 3 gm Pr, 21 gm Ca, 315 mg So, 1 Fi
DIABETIC: 1 St, 1 Fa

South-of-the-Border Beans

My son James thought these tasted better than refried beans! He said they had more flavor and weren't greasy at all. It's the salsa that performs that magic. ●   Serves 6

> 20 ounces (two 16-ounce cans) Great Northern or white
>   beans, rinsed and drained
> ³/₄ cup chunky salsa
> 1 tablespoon Healthy Choice or Heinz Lite ketchup
> 1 tablespoon Brown Sugar Twin
> ¹/₂ teaspoon dried parsley flakes
> ¹/₈ teaspoon black pepper
> ³/₄ cup (3 ounces) Kraft shredded reduced-fat Cheddar
>   cheese

Preheat oven to 350 degrees. In a medium saucepan, warm beans. Add salsa and ketchup. Mix in Brown Sugar Twin, parsley flakes, and black pepper. Add Cheddar cheese. Mix well to combine. Pour into an 8-by-8-inch baking dish sprayed with olive-flavored cooking spray. Bake 20 to 30 minutes.

Each serving equals:

HE: 2¹/₃ Pr, ¹/₄ Ve, 4 OC
155 Calories, 2 gm Fa, 12 gm Pr, 22 gm Ca, 260 mg So, 1 Fi
DIABETIC: 1¹/₂ St, 1 Mt

Party Potatoes

These creamy, cheesy potatoes are a perfect excuse for a party, or a delicious dish to serve to family and friends. Your taste buds will thank you! ○   Serves 8

> 8 cups (25 ounces) frozen shredded potatoes, thawed, or raw shredded potatoes
> 1 cup (one 4-ounce can) canned sliced mushrooms, drained
> 3 tablespoons dried onion flakes
> 1½ cups (one 12-fluid-ounce can) Carnation evaporated skim milk
> ⅓ cup Carnation nonfat dry milk powder
> 3 tablespoons flour
> 1 teaspoon dried parsley flakes
> ⅛ teaspoon black pepper
> 1½ cups (6 ounces) Kraft shredded reduced-fat Cheddar cheese

Spray an 8-by-12-inch baking dish with butter-flavored cooking spray. In a large bowl, combine potatoes, mushrooms, and dried onion flakes. In a small bowl, combine evaporated skim milk, dry milk powder, flour, parsley flakes, and black pepper. Add to potato mixture. Mix well to combine. Pour into baking dish. Top with Cheddar cheese. Cover and let set in refrigerator for at least 1 hour. Bake 30 minutes in a 350-degree oven.

Each serving equals:

HE: 1 Pr, ¾ Br, ½ SM, ¼ Ve

185 Calories, 3 gm Fa, 13 gm Pr, 27 gm Ca, 325 mg So, 2 Fi

DIABETIC: 2 St, 1 Mt

Main Dishes

P art of the Healthy Exchanges® approach to creating meals is understanding how the main dish—the centerpiece of the meal— has changed. We used to expect a big piece of meat plus potatoes and vegetables swimming in butter, but now we're cutting down our fat and cholesterol and paying more attention to calories and portion sizes. The dishes we choose to serve emphasize more pasta, rice, potatoes, and vegetables, and smaller servings of protein. But Healthy Exchanges® recipes still provide delicious flavor and "mouth" appeal. If you thought that foods like Fettuccine Alfredo or Tamale Pie were just fond memories, if you can't face another dry chicken breast or piece of plain broiled fish, take some time to read the recipes in this Main Dishes section. I've eliminated the extra fat and calories in many family favorites but kept the great tastes and textures of the "real thing." With entrees like these, every meal can be a celebration of good, healthy eating!

Fettuccine Alfredo

My daughter-in-law Pam is the Alfredo lover in the family. She told me this was as good as any she's eaten in a restaurant. (Thanks, Pam!) If you love creamy pastas but have avoided them because of the fat, here's your chance to eat what you like—and stay healthy. ☻ Serves 4 (⅔ cup)

⅓ cup Carnation nonfat dry milk powder
½ cup warm water
2 tablespoons + 2 teaspoons reduced-calorie margarine
¾ cup (2¼ ounces) grated Kraft House Italian or Parmesan
  cheese
2 cups hot cooked fettuccine

In a large bowl, combine dry milk powder and warm water. Add reduced-calorie margarine and House Italian cheese. Mix well until blended. Add hot fettuccine and toss to coat. Serve at once.

Hint: 1½ cups uncooked fettuccine usually make 2 cups cooked.

Each serving equals:
HE: 1 Br, 1 Fa, 1 Pr, ¼ SM
223 Calories, 7 gm Fa, 13 gm Pr, 27 gm Ca, 330 mg So, 1 Fi
DIABETIC: 1½ St, 1 Fa, 1 Mt

Cheesy Macaroni- Vegetable Bake

Adding vegetables and Dijon mustard to this "old standby" transforms it—and makes a bland, "old news" dish into "new news!" ● Serves 4

> *2 cups cooked elbow macaroni, rinsed and drained*
> *2 cups frozen carrot, broccoli, and cauliflower blend*
> *vegetables, cooked and drained*
> *²/₃ cup Carnation nonfat dry milk powder*
> *1 cup water*
> *1 tablespoon Dijon mustard*
> *³/₄ cup (3 ounces) Kraft shredded reduced-fat*
> *Cheddar cheese*
> *³/₄ cup (3 ounces) Kraft shredded reduced-fat*
> *mozzarella cheese*
> *¹/₈ teaspoon lemon pepper*

Preheat oven to 350 degrees. In a large bowl, combine macaroni and vegetables. In a small bowl, combine dry milk powder and water. Add to macaroni mixture. Stir in mustard, Cheddar and mozzarella cheeses, and lemon pepper. Mix well to combine. Spray an 8-by-8-inch baking dish with butter-flavored cooking spray. Pour mixture into dish. Bake 30 minutes.

Hints: 1. 1³/₄ cups uncooked elbow macaroni usually make about 2 cups cooked.
2. 1 cup frozen carrots, ¹/₂ cup frozen cauliflower, and ¹/₂ cup frozen broccoli can be used in place of blended vegetables.

Each serving equals:

HE: 2 Pr, 1 Br, 1 Ve, ¹/₂ SM

274 Calories, 7 gm Fa, 21 gm Pr, 31 gm Ca, 569 mg So, 2 Fi

DIABETIC: 2 Mt, 1 St, 1 Ve, ¹/₂ SM

Mexican Rice

Easy. Tasty. Filling. What more could you ask from a meatless main-dish recipe that is bound to be a regular on your table?

○ Serves 4

½ cup chopped onion
2 cups chunky salsa
⅛ teaspoon black pepper
2 cups cooked rice
1 cup (3¾ ounces) Kraft shredded reduced-fat
  Cheddar cheese ☆

Preheat oven to 350 degrees. In a skillet sprayed with olive-flavored cooking spray, sauté onion until tender, about 5 minutes. Add salsa and black pepper. Mix in rice and ¾ cup Cheddar cheese. Stir until cheese is melted. Pour into an 8-by-8-inch baking dish sprayed with olive-flavored cooking spray. Bake 15 minutes. Sprinkle remaining ¼ cup Cheddar cheese on top and bake an additional 5 minutes or until cheese melts.

Hint: 1⅓ cups uncooked rice usually make about 2 cups cooked.

Each serving equals:

HE: 1¼ Pr, 1¼ Ve, 1 Br

149 Calories, 3 gm Fa, 9 gm Pr, 21 gm Ca, 655 mg So, 1 Fi

DIABETIC: 1 Mt, 1 Ve, 1 St

Rice Primavera

Did you know that "primavera" means spring? Well, this attractive dish will convince you it's spring, no matter what the weather is doing outside. ❍   Serves 4 (1 full cup)

> 1 tablespoon + 1 teaspoon reduced-calorie margarine
> 2 cups (one 16-ounce can) Campbell's Healthy Request
>   Chicken Broth
> 1 teaspoon dried basil leaves
> ½ cup finely chopped onion
> 1 cup frozen sliced carrots
> 1 cup frozen green beans
> 1⅓ cups (4 ounces) uncooked instant rice
> ½ cup (1½ ounces) grated Kraft House Italian or Parmesan
>   cheese

In a medium saucepan, combine margarine, chicken broth, basil, onion, carrots, and green beans. Bring mixture to a boil. Cover and simmer until vegetables are tender, about 10 minutes. Stir in rice. Cover. Remove from heat. Let stand 5 minutes or until all broth is absorbed. Stir in House Italian cheese and fluff with a fork before serving.

Each serving equals:

HE: 1¼ Ve, 1 Br, ½ Pr, ½ Fa, 8 OC
204 Calories, 5 gm Fa, 9 gm Pr, 31 gm Ca, 463 mg So, 3 Fi
DIABETIC: 1½ St, 1 Ve, ½ Mt, ½ Fa

Fried Rice with Ham

Yes—you *can* have fried rice when it's prepared the Healthy Exchanges® way! Isn't that great news? ☻   Serves 4 (¾ cup)

2 eggs, beaten, or equivalent in egg substitute
1 teaspoon vegetable oil
½ cup (3 ounces) diced Dubuque 97% fat-free or any extra-lean ham
¼ cup sliced green onion
¼ cup shredded carrot
¼ cup frozen peas, thawed
1¾ cups cooked rice
4 teaspoons reduced-sodium soy sauce
⅛ teaspoon black pepper

Place eggs in a skillet or wok sprayed with butter-flavored cooking spray. Using a spatula, lift eggs as they cook, letting uncooked part run underneath until set. Transfer eggs to cutting board and cut into shreds. Pour vegetable oil into skillet or wok set on medium-high heat. Add ham, onion, carrots, and peas. Stir-fry about 1 minute. Add shredded eggs, rice, soy sauce, and black pepper, stirring until heated through.

Hint: 1¼ cups uncooked rice usually make about 1¾ cups cooked.

Each serving equals:

HE: 1 Pr (½ limited), 1 Br, ¼ Fa, ¼ Ve
153 Calories, 5 gm Fa, 9 gm Pr, 18 gm Ca, 240 mg So, 2 Fi
DIABETIC: 1 Mt, 1 St

Creamy Potato-Ham Bake

I created this dish for my own "meat and potatoes" man, Cliff. He said to tell you that this met his high standards—and passed with flying colors. ● Serves 6

> 4½ cups (15 ounces) frozen shredded potatoes, thawed, or
>   raw shredded potatoes
> 1½ cups frozen peas
> 1 full cup (6 ounces) diced Dubuque 97% fat-free or any
>   extra-lean ham
> ½ teaspoon dried parsley flakes
> ¼ teaspoon black pepper
> 1 (10¾-ounce) can Campbell's Healthy Request Cream of
>   Mushroom Soup

Preheat oven to 350 degrees. In a large bowl, combine potatoes, peas, and ham. In a small bowl combine parsley flakes, black pepper, and mushroom soup. Pour soup mixture over potato mixture. Mix well to combine. Pour into an 8-by-8-inch baking dish sprayed with butter-flavored cooking spray. Bake 25 to 30 minutes.

Each serving equals:

HE: 1 Br, ⅔ Pr, ¼ Sl, 8 OC

139 Calories, 2 gm Fa, 8 gm Pr, 22 gm Ca, 496 mg So, 3 Fi

DIABETIC: 1½ St, 1 Mt

Rio Grande Potatoes

One bite of this easy dish, and you'll see why it's called "grande"—rich taste and lots of flavor. I leave the degree of heat of the salsa to your own preference. ● Serves 4

4 cups (20 ounces) unpeeled baking potatoes, thickly sliced
8 ounces ground 90% lean turkey or beef
1 cup chunky salsa
¼ cup Land O Lakes fat-free sour cream
½ cup (2¼ ounces) Kraft shredded reduced-fat Cheddar
cheese

Preheat oven to 350 degrees. Place potatoes in an 8-by-8-inch baking dish. Spray potatoes with butter-flavored cooking spray. Bake until tender, about 30 to 45 minutes. In a skillet sprayed with olive-flavored cooking spray, brown meat. Stir in salsa. Lower heat. Simmer until meat and potatoes are cooked through. When serving place ¼ of potatoes on each serving plate. Spoon meat mixture evenly over potatoes. Top each with 1 tablespoon sour cream and about 2 tablespoons Cheddar cheese.

Each serving equals:

HE: 2¼ Pr, 1 Br, ½ Ve, 15 OC
255 Calories, 7 gm Fa, 19 gm Pr, 29 gm Ca, 440 mg So, 2 Fi
DIABETIC: 2 Mt, 2 St

All-American Casserole

Wave the flag for our great nation when you enjoy the bounty of the earth in this filling dish. Declare your independence from fat without giving up any of the great taste you enjoy.

● Serves 4

> 8 ounces ground 90% lean turkey or beef
> ½ cup chopped onion
> 3 full cups (10 ounces) frozen shredded potatoes, thawed, or raw shredded potatoes
> 2 cups (one 16-ounce can) canned sliced carrots, rinsed and drained
> 1¾ cups (one 15-ounce can) Hunt's Chunky Tomato Sauce
> ⅛ teaspoon lemon pepper
> 1 teaspoon dried basil or 1 tablespoon finely chopped fresh basil
> 1 cup frozen peas
> ¾ cup (3 ounces) Kraft shredded reduced-fat Cheddar cheese

Preheat oven to 350 degrees. In a skillet sprayed with butter-flavored cooking spray, sauté meat and onion until browned. In a large mixing bowl combine potatoes, carrots, tomato sauce, lemon pepper, and basil. Mix in meat mixture, peas, and Cheddar cheese. Pour into an 8-by-8-inch baking dish sprayed with butter-flavored cooking spray. Bake 20 to 30 minutes or until cheese is melted through.

Each serving equals:
    HE: 3 Ve, 2¼ Pr, 1 Br
    281 Calories, 9 gm Fa, 20 gm Pr, 31 gm Ca, 1,002 mg So, 6 Fi
    DIABETIC: 2 Mt, 2 Ve, 1½ St

Barbecue Biscuit Cups

I haven't met a kid yet who hasn't enjoyed this easy dinner treat—and I meet kids of *all* ages. Just add a tossed salad and green beans prepared "your way" and your work is done for a fun-time meal. ❂ Serves 5 (2 cups each)

8 ounces ground 90% lean turkey or beef
¼ cup chopped green bell pepper
⅓ cup finely chopped onion
1 cup (one 8-ounce can) Hunt's Tomato Sauce
1 tablespoon Brown Sugar Twin
1 teaspoon prepared mustard
⅛ teaspoon black pepper
1 (7.5-ounce) can Pillsbury refrigerated flaky biscuits
½ cup full (2¼ ounces) Kraft shredded reduced-fat Cheddar
 cheese

Preheat oven to 400 degrees. In a large skillet sprayed with olive-flavored cooking spray, brown ground meat, green pepper, and onions. Add tomato sauce, Brown Sugar Twin, mustard, and black pepper. Simmer 5 minutes. Place each biscuit in an ungreased muffin cup, pressing dough up sides to edge of cup. Evenly spoon meat mixture into cups. Bake 10 to 15 minutes or until golden brown. Sprinkle with Cheddar cheese and continue to bake 2 to 3 minutes or until cheese melts.

Each serving equals:

HE: 1½ Br, 1½ Pr, 1 Ve, 1 OC
270 Calories, 10 gm Fa, 16 gm Pr, 25 gm Ca, 873 mg So, 2 Fi
DIABETIC: 1½ St, 1½ Mt, 1 Ve

Cabbage and Rice Casserole

After I create and perfect a recipe, I usually don't prepare it again because I'm on to new ideas. I shared this recipe with a few people and forgot about it. About a year later, I attended a potluck and tried a spoonful of a wonderful cabbage and rice dish. After tracking down the person who brought it, I found out it was *my* recipe! ◯   Serves 4

> 8 ounces ground 90% lean turkey or beef
>
> 2 cups coarsely chopped cabbage
>
> ½ cup chopped onion
>
> ⅔ cup (2 ounces) uncooked regular rice
>
> 3 cups (one 28-ounce can) canned tomatoes, chopped fine,
>   with juice
>
> 2 teaspoons prepared mustard
>
> 2 tablespoons Brown Sugar Twin
>
> ⅛ teaspoon lemon pepper

Preheat oven to 350 degrees. In a large skillet sprayed with butter-flavored cooking spray, brown meat. Spray an 8-by-8-inch baking dish with butter-flavored cooking spray. Layer cabbage on bottom of dish. Cover with onion, browned meat, and rice. In a small bowl, combine chopped tomatoes with juice, mustard, Brown Sugar Twin, and lemon pepper. Pour tomato mixture over rice. Cover and bake 1½ hours. Uncover and bake an additional 10 minutes.

Each serving equals:

HE: 2¾ Ve, 1½ Pr, ½ Br, 2 OC

193 Calories, 5 gm Fa, 14 gm Pr, 23 gm Ca, 390 mg So, 3 Fi

DIABETIC: 1½ Mt, 1 Ve, 1 St

Chili Jackpot Casserole

You will think you hit the jackpot when you try this easy casserole. It's really just tasty chili with pasta and Cheddar cheese added to make it a real winner! ● Serves 6

8 ounces ground 90% lean turkey or beef
¹/₄ cup chopped green bell pepper
¹/₄ cup chopped onion
1¹/₂ teaspoons chili seasoning mix
¹/₄ teaspoon black pepper
1³/₄ cups (one 15-ounce can) Hunt's Chunky Tomato Sauce
3 cups cooked rotini pasta, rinsed and drained
10 ounces (one 16-ounce can) canned red kidney beans,
*   rinsed and drained*
1 scant cup (3³/₄ ounces) Kraft shredded reduced-fat
*   Cheddar cheese ☆*

Preheat oven to 350 degrees. In a large skillet sprayed with olive-flavored cooking spray, brown meat, green pepper, and onion. Add chili seasoning mix and black pepper. Mix well. Stir in tomato sauce, rotini pasta, kidney beans, and ¹/₂ cup Cheddar cheese. Mix well to combine. Pour into an 8-by-8-inch baking dish sprayed with olive-flavored cooking spray. Sprinkle remaining ¹/₂ cup Cheddar cheese over top. Bake 20 minutes or until cheese melts.

Hint: 2¹/₂ cups dry rotini pasta usually make 3 cups cooked.

Each serving equals:

HE: 2²/₃ Pr, 1¹/₃ Ve, 1 Br
261 Calories, 7 gm Fa, 19 gm Pr, 31 gm Ca, 583 mg So, 3 Fi
DIABETIC: 2 Mt, 2 St

Deep-Dish Pizza

If you thought you had to give up pizza just because you want to eat healthy, think again. This very filling pizza is almost as quick to make as it is to have a pizza delivered. And while my version delivers plenty of flavor, it leaves the excess fats behind.

○ Serves 12 (1 piece)

> 16 ounces ground 90% lean turkey or beef
> ½ cup chopped onion
> 1 teaspoon dried parsley flakes
> ¼ teaspoon minced garlic
> 3 cups Bisquick reduced-fat baking mix
> ¾ cup water
> 1½ teaspoons pizza spice or Italian seasoning
> 1¾ cups (one 15-ounce can) Hunt's Chunky Tomato Sauce
> 1 cup (one 4-ounce can) canned sliced mushrooms, drained
> 1 cup chopped green bell pepper
> 1½ cups (6 ounces) Kraft shredded reduced-fat mozzarella
>   cheese

Preheat oven to 425 degrees. In a large skillet sprayed with olive-flavored cooking spray, brown meat and onion. Add parsley flakes and garlic. Spray an 11-by-16-inch jelly-roll pan with olive-flavored cooking spray. In a large bowl, combine baking mix and water until soft ball is formed. Place dough on wax paper and knead 20 times. Pat dough in bottom of pan and up sides. Add Italian seasoning to tomato sauce. Spread sauce over dough. Spoon meat mixture over sauce. Top with mushrooms, green pepper, and mozzarella cheese. Bake 20 minutes. Cut into 12 pieces.

Each serving equals:

HE: 1⅔ Pr, 1⅓ Br, 1 Ve

214 Calories, 8 gm Fa, 14 gm Pr, 22 gm Ca, 568 mg So, 2 Fi

DIABETIC: 2 Mt, 1 St, 1 Ve, 1 Free Ve

Impossible Lasagna

No, this lasagna is not impossible to make . . . it just seems that it's impossible to have this much flavor in such a healthy preparation. You know how they say in the Army that "the difficult we do immediately, the impossible takes a little longer"? Well, this recipe, start to finish, takes just over 30 minutes.

○   Serves 6

8 ounces ground 90% lean turkey
   or beef
1/2 cup fat-free cottage cheese
1/4 cup (3/4 ounce) grated Kraft
   House Italian or Parmesan
   cheese
2 teaspoons Italian seasoning
1 cup (one 8-ounce can)
   Hunt's Tomato Sauce
3/4 cup (3 ounces) Kraft shredded
   reduced-fat mozzarella
   cheese ☆

1 cup skim milk
1/3 cup Carnation nonfat dry milk
   powder
9 tablespoons Bisquick reduced-
   fat baking mix
2 eggs or equivalent in egg
   substitute
1/2 teaspoon salt
1/8 teaspoon black pepper

Preheat oven to 400 degrees. In a large skillet sprayed with olive-flavored cooking spray, brown meat. Spray an 8-by-8-inch baking dish with olive-flavored cooking spray. Layer cottage cheese and House Italian cheese on bottom. Add Italian seasoning, tomato sauce, and 1/4 cup of the mozzarella cheese to browned meat. Spoon over cheese layer. In a blender combine skim milk, dry milk powder, baking mix, eggs, salt, and black pepper for 15 seconds on HIGH speed. Pour over meat mixture. Bake 30 minutes. Spread remaining 1/2 cup mozzarella cheese on top and bake an additional 5 minutes. Let set 5 minutes before cutting.

Each serving equals:

HE: 2 1/3 Pr (1/3 limited), 2/3 Ve, 1/2 Br, 1/3 SM
229 Calories, 9 gm Fa, 21 gm Pr, 15 gm Ca, 752 mg So, 1 Fi
DIABETIC: 3 Mt, 1 St

Mexicalli Pie

This is the recipe that started the whole thing, that launched Healthy Exchanges®. It's the first one I ever created—and when I served it to Cliff, he told me he would eat anything else I prepared, no matter how healthy, as long as it tasted this good! That's about as high a compliment as a truck-drivin' man can give.

● Serves 8

16 ounces ground 90% lean turkey or beef
½ cup chopped onion
½ cup chopped green and/or red bell peppers
1½ cups frozen corn
1 cup chunky salsa
¾ cup (3 ounces) Kraft shredded reduced-fat Cheddar
   cheese
⅛ teaspoon black pepper
1 cup (3 ounces) crushed corn chips

Preheat oven to 350 degrees. In a large skillet sprayed with olive-flavored cooking spray, brown meat, onions, and green pepper. Add corn, salsa, Cheddar cheese, and black pepper. Spray a 10-inch pie plate with olive-flavored cooking spray. Place meat mixture in pie plate. Top with crushed corn chips. Bake 30 minutes. Cool 10 minutes before serving.

Each serving equals:

HE: 2 Pr, ¾ Br, ½ Ve, ¼ Sl, 10 OC
204 Calories, 10 gm Fa, 15 gm Pr, 14 gm Ca, 324 mg So, 2 Fi
DIABETIC: 2 Mt, 1 St

Meat Loaf with Vegetable Stuffing

I think you will be very pleased with this combination of meat loaf and vegetables. It even satisfies those "meat and potato" folks!

○ Serves 6

½ cup (one 2.5-ounce jar) canned sliced mushrooms, drained

1 cup (one 8-ounce can) canned carrots, rinsed, drained, and chopped

1 cup (one 8-ounce can) canned green beans, rinsed, drained, and chopped

3 tablespoons (¾ ounce) dried fine bread crumbs

2 eggs or equivalent in egg substitute ☆

16 ounces ground 90% lean turkey or beef

½ cup chopped onion

½ cup (1½ ounces) rolled oats

1 tablespoon Worcestershire sauce

¼ cup Healthy Choice or Heinz Lite ketchup

¼ teaspoon black pepper

½ teaspoon garlic powder

Preheat oven to 375 degrees. In a medium bowl, combine mushrooms, carrots, green beans, bread crumbs, and 1 egg. Set aside. In a large bowl, combine meat, onion, oats, remaining egg, Worcestershire sauce, ketchup, black pepper, and garlic powder. Spread half of meat mixture in bottom of ungreased 9-by-5-inch loaf pan. Cover with vegetable mixture, spreading evenly. Spread remaining half of meat mixture over vegetables. Bake 45 to 55 minutes. Cool 10 minutes before serving.

Each serving equals:

HE: 2⅓ Pr (⅓ limited), 1 Ve, ½ Br, 10 OC

211 Calories, 9 gm Fa, 18 gm Pr, 15 gm Ca, 442 mg So, 2 Fi

DIABETIC: 2 Mt, 1 Ve, 1 St

Pizza Casserole

Mothers all over the country have reported back to me that this easy casserole makes a big hit with their teenagers. It's simple enough for the kids to make all by themselves, so you can relax before dinner—well, it's a nice thought, anyway. ☻ Serves 6

8 ounces ground 90% lean turkey or beef
½ cup chopped onion
3 cups cooked noodles, rinsed and drained
⅓ full cup (2 ounces) thin-sliced pepperoni, chopped
1¾ cups (one 15-ounce can) Hunt's Chunky Tomato Sauce
1 cup (one 4-ounce can) canned sliced mushrooms, drained
1 teaspoon pizza spice or Italian seasoning
¾ cup (3 ounces) Kraft shredded reduced-fat mozzarella
*   cheese*

Preheat oven to 350 degrees. In a large skillet sprayed with olive-flavored cooking spray, brown meat and onion. Stir in noodles, pepperoni, tomato sauce, mushrooms, and seasoning. Mix well. Pour into an ungreased 8-by-8-inch baking dish. Bake 20 minutes. Sprinkle top with mozzarella cheese. Bake an additional 5 minutes or until cheese melts.

Hint: 2⅔ cups uncooked noodles usually make 3 cups cooked.

Each serving equals:

HE: 2 Pr (⅓ limited), 1⅔ Ve, 1 Br⁓
282 Calories, 11 gm Fa, 18 gm Pr, 28 gm Ca, 893 mg So, 3 Fi
DIABETIC: 2 Mt, 2 Ve, 1 St

Salisbury Steak

This meat loaf is all dressed up and ready to "party," but even if your only guests are your family, they'll thank you for serving this tasty, tangy dish. ☻ Serves 4

> 6 tablespoons (1½ ounces) dried fine bread crumbs
> 8 ounces ground 90% lean turkey or beef
> 1 egg or equivalent in egg substitute
> ⅛ teaspoon black pepper
> ½ cup chopped onion
> 2 tablespoons Worcestershire sauce
> 3 tablespoons Healthy Choice or Heinz Lite ketchup
> 1 (10¾-ounce) can Campbell's Healthy Request Cream of
>   Mushroom Soup

Preheat oven to 350 degrees. In a medium bowl, combine bread crumbs, meat, egg, black pepper, and onion. Form into 4 patties. Place in a hot skillet sprayed with butter-flavored cooking spray. Brown patties on both sides. Place browned patties in an 8-by-8-inch baking dish. In a small bowl, combine Worcestershire sauce, ketchup, and mushroom soup. Pour over patties. Bake 30 minutes.

Each serving equals:
    HE: 1¾ Pr (¼ limited), ½ Br, ¼ Ve, ½ Sl, 13 OC
    210 Calories, 8 gm Fa, 14 gm Pr, 20 gm Ca, 697 mg So, 1 Fi
    DIABETIC: 2 Mt, 1 St

Taco Casserole

If this easy casserole doesn't satisfy the Mexican food lovers in your household, I don't know what will. Remember, if you're like Cliff and love the feel of smoke coming out of your ears, just add more taco seasoning. But if you're a wimp like me, stick with the amount suggested. ☻   Serves 4

> 8 ounces ground 90% lean turkey or beef
> ½ cup chopped onion
> ½ cup chopped green bell pepper
> 1¾ cups (one 15-ounce can) Hunt's Chunky Tomato Sauce
> 1 tablespoon taco seasoning mix
> 2 cups cooked noodles, rinsed and drained
> ¾ cup (3 ounces) Kraft shredded reduced-fat Cheddar
>   cheese

Preheat oven to 350 degrees. In a large skillet sprayed with olive-flavored cooking spray, brown meat, onion, and green pepper. Add tomato sauce and taco seasoning. Simmer 5 to 10 minutes. Stir in cooked noodles. Pour into an 8-by-8-inch baking dish sprayed with olive-flavored cooking spray. Bake 15 to 20 minutes. Top with Cheddar cheese and bake another 10 minutes or until cheese melts. Let set 5 minutes before serving.

Hint: A full 1¾ cups uncooked noodles usually make about 2 cups cooked.

Each serving equals:

HE: 2½ Pr, 2¼ Ve, 1 Br
295 Calories, 10 gm Fa, 21 gm Pr, 31 gm Ca, 828 mg So, 3 Fi
DIABETIC: 2 Mt, 2 Ve, 1 St

Tamale Pie

Hot tamale! This one will definitely hit the spot when a South-of-the-Border hunger attack strikes. ● Serves 6

1½ cups water
4 teaspoons reduced-calorie margarine
1 (6-serving) package Stove Top corn-bread stuffing mix
8 ounces ground 90% lean turkey or beef
½ cup chopped green bell pepper
½ cup chopped onion
¼ cup (1 ounce) sliced black olives
1¾ cups (one 15-ounce can) Hunt's Chunky Tomato Sauce
2 teaspoons chili seasoning mix
¾ cup (3 ounces) Kraft shredded reduced-fat Cheddar
   cheese

Preheat oven to 350 degrees. In a medium saucepan, combine water and margarine. Bring mixture to a boil. Simmer 5 minutes. Remove from heat. Add dry corn-bread mix. Mix well to combine. In a large skillet sprayed with olive-flavored cooking spray, brown meat, green pepper, and onion. Add olives, tomato sauce, and chili seasoning. Stir in Cheddar cheese. Mix well to combine. Pour into an 8-by-8-inch baking dish. Spread prepared stuffing mix on top of meat mixture. Bake 20 to 25 minutes.

Each serving equals:
   HE: 1⅔ Pr, 1½ Ve, 1 Br, ½ Fa, ¼ Sl, 10 OC
   253 Calories, 9 gm Fa, 15 gm Pr, 29 gm Ca, 954 mg So, 3 Fi
   DIABETIC: 2 Ve, 1½ Mt, 1 St, ½ Fa

Healthy Jo's™

Here's my version of the old standby. It's an easy meal to make for a crowd, or perfect for those weekend suppers in front of the TV when a favorite movie is on. Cliff says he could eat this every week and never get tired of it. The husband of one of my readers says it's the *second*-best thing they do together all week long!

○ Serves 6 (⅓ cup filling)

> *6 reduced-calorie hamburger buns*
> *16 ounces ground 90% lean turkey or beef*
> *½ cup chopped onion*
> *1 cup (one 8-ounce can) Hunt's Tomato Sauce*
> *½ cup chunky salsa*
> *1 tablespoon Brown Sugar Twin*

In a large skillet sprayed with olive-flavored cooking spray, brown meat and onion. Add tomato sauce, salsa, and Brown Sugar Twin. Lower heat and simmer 15 to 20 minutes. Serve on hamburger buns.

Each serving equals:

HE: 2 Pr, 1 Br, 1 Ve, 1 OC

209 Calories, 7 gm Fa, 17 gm Pr, 19 gm Ca, 567 mg So, 2 Fi

DIABETIC: 2 Mt, 1 St, 1 Ve

Mexican "Swiss" Steak

You choose how much heat you enjoy in your Mexican dishes. Cliff always goes for the extra-hot salsa, while I prefer a milder version. I read somewhere that spicy food is supposed to make you burn more calories. If it does, maybe Cliff has the right idea!

○   Serves 4

> 1 tablespoon flour
> 1 tablespoon chili seasoning mix
> 4 (4-ounce) lean minute beef steaks
> 1¾ cups (one 15-ounce can) Hunt's Chunky Tomato Sauce
> ½ cup chunky salsa

In a flat dish combine flour and chili seasoning mix. Gently coat steaks. Spray a large skillet with olive-flavored cooking spray. Brown steaks on both sides over medium heat. In a medium bowl, combine tomato sauce and salsa. Pour sauce mixture over steaks. Lower heat. Cover and simmer 20 to 30 minutes.

Hint: This tomato salsa sauce is also good over rice, potatoes, or pasta.

Each serving equals:

HE: 3 Pr, 2 Ve, 8 OC

245 Calories, 10 gm Fa, 28 gm Pr, 10 gm Ca, 764 mg So, 2 Fi

DIABETIC: 3 Mt, 2 Ve

Truck Stop Biscuits and Gravy

Cliff said these were every bit as good as any he had during his years on the road in his 18-wheeler—and that he would pull into my kitchen anytime I promised to serve him these.

⊘   Serves 5 (2 biscuits and ¾ cup gravy)

> 1 (7.5-ounce) can Pillsbury refrigerated buttermilk biscuits
> 8 ounces ground 90% lean turkey or beef
> ¼ teaspoon black pepper
> ¼ teaspoon ground sage
> ¼ teaspoon garlic powder
> ¼ teaspoon poultry seasoning
> 2½ cups skim milk
> ¼ cup flour
> 1 (8-ounce) package Philadelphia fat-free cream cheese

Bake biscuits according to package directions. Meanwhile, in a large skillet sprayed with butter-flavored cooking spray, brown meat. Add black pepper, sage, garlic powder, and poultry seasoning. In a covered jar, combine skim milk and flour. Shake well. Pour milk mixture into skillet with browned meat. Add cream cheese. Continue cooking, stirring often, until mixture thickens and cream cheese melts. When serving, spoon gravy over biscuits.

Each serving equals:

HE: 2 Pr, 1¾ Br, ½ SM

287 Calories, 8 gm Fa, 21 gm Pr, 32 gm Ca, 876 mg So, 2 Fi

DIABETIC: 2 Mt, 2 St, ½ SM

Roast Beef Rolls

This simple-to-prepare dish is a pleasant change of pace from traditional roast beef dishes. Isn't it great to know that you don't have to give up eating beef if you enjoy it? Now that it's possible to buy extra-lean beef, we can still enjoy the foods we love—in moderation. ☻ Serves 4 (2 each)

1 cup minced fresh mushrooms
1 cup finely diced onion
1 tablespoon + 1 teaspoon reduced-calorie margarine
8 slices (approximately ½ ounce each) cold lean cooked
   roast beef, sliced very thin
¼ cup Kraft fat-free Thousand Island dressing

Preheat oven to 350 degrees. In a medium skillet sauté mushrooms and onion in margarine until lightly browned. Spread equal amounts of mushroom-and-onion mixture on roast beef slices. Roll each slice of beef and place seam side down in 8-by-12-inch baking dish sprayed with butter-flavored cooking spray. Spoon dressing evenly over beef rolls. Bake 10 minutes or until rolls are heated through. Serve immediately.

Hint: Purchase roast beef from deli and have them slice it for you.

Each serving equals:

HE: 1 Pr, 1 Ve, ½ Fa, ¼ Sl
100 Calories, 3 gm Fa, 9 gm Pr, 9 gm Ca, 167 mg So, 1 Fi
DIABETIC: 1 Mt, 1 Ve

Potatoes Olé

This "meat and potatoes" dish quickly became a favorite with the men in my household. Cliff, James, and Tommy all said *Olé* and asked for second helpings. Isn't it amazing?　●　Serves 4

> ½ cup chopped onion
> 3 full cups (10 ounces) frozen shredded potatoes, thawed, or raw shredded potatoes
> 1 cup (one 8-ounce can) canned sliced carrots, rinsed and drained
> 1 cup (one 8-ounce can) canned sliced green beans, rinsed and drained
> 1 (10¾-ounce) can Campbell's Healthy Request Cream of Mushroom Soup
> 1 cup chunky salsa
> 1 scant cup (4 ounces) diced lean cooked roast beef
> ¾ cup (3 ounces) Kraft shredded reduced-fat Cheddar cheese
> ½ teaspoon lemon pepper

Preheat oven to 350 degrees. In a skillet sprayed with olive-flavored cooking spray, brown onions. Add potatoes, carrots, green beans, mushroom soup, salsa, beef, Cheddar cheese, and lemon pepper. Mix well. Spray an 8-by-8-inch baking dish with olive-flavored cooking spray. Pour mixture into dish. Bake 45 minutes.

Hint: If you don't have leftovers, purchase a chunk of cooked lean roast beef from your local deli.

Each serving equals:

HE: 2 Pr, 1¾ Ve, ½ Br, ½ Sl, 10 OC
232 Calories, 6 gm Fa, 18 gm Pr, 26 gm Ca, 1,043 mg So, 3 Fi
DIABETIC: 2 Mt, 2 Ve, 1 St

Chicken Pot Casserole

This is my contribution to the "chicken in every pot" promised us so many years ago. It has the flavor of a traditional pot pie but without all the work—or all the fat. Serve this to your family, then stand back and enjoy the applause. ☻ Serves 4

2 cups cooked noodles, rinsed
    and drained
½ cup chopped onion
1 full cup (6 ounces) diced
    cooked chicken breast
1 cup frozen carrots, thawed
1 cup frozen green beans, thawed
½ cup frozen peas, thawed
½ cup (one 2.5-ounce jar)
    canned sliced mushrooms,
    drained

1 (10¾-ounce) can Campbell's
    Healthy Request Cream of
    Mushroom Soup
½ teaspoon poultry seasoning
⅛ teaspoon black pepper
1 teaspoon dried parsley flakes
⅓ cup (1½ ounces) Kraft
    shredded reduced-fat
    Cheddar cheese
3 tablespoons (¾ ounce) dried
    fine bread crumbs

Preheat oven to 350 degrees. In a large bowl, combine noodles, onion, chicken, carrots, green beans, peas, mushrooms, mushroom soup, poultry seasoning, black pepper, and parsley. Pour into an ungreased 8-by-8-inch baking dish. Bake 15 to 20 minutes or until hot. Sprinkle Cheddar cheese and bread crumbs on top and bake an additional 5 minutes or until cheese melts.

Hints: 1. A full 1¾ cups uncooked noodles usually make about 2 cups cooked.
            2. Purchase cooked chicken breast from your local deli and dice it when you get home.

Each serving equals:
    HE: 2 Pr, 1½ Br, 1½ Ve, ½ Sl, 1 OC
    297 Calories, 6 gm Fa, 22 gm Pr, 38 gm Ca, 576 mg So, 4 Fi
    DIABETIC: 2 Mt, 2 St, 1 Ve

Chicken-Rice-Broccoli Bake

My daughter, Becky, loves the combination of chicken, rice, and broccoli, so it was only natural that I revise an old family favorite and create a new dish that still meets with her approval. With the almonds and cheese, this tastes like a special party dish—but you can enjoy it anytime.   ●   Serves 4

> 2 cups cooked rice
> 1 scant cup (4 ounces) diced cooked chicken breast
> 2 cups frozen cut broccoli, cooked and drained
> 1/4 cup (1 ounce) sliced almonds
> 2/3 cup Carnation nonfat dry milk powder
> 1 cup water
> 1/3 cup (1 1/2 ounces) Kraft shredded reduced-fat
>   Cheddar cheese
> 1/8 teaspoon lemon pepper
> 2 tablespoons reduced-sodium soy sauce

Preheat oven to 350 degrees. In a medium bowl, combine rice, chicken, broccoli, and almonds. In a small bowl, combine dry milk powder and water. Add Cheddar cheese, lemon pepper, and soy sauce. Mix well to combine. Pour cheese mixture into rice mixture. Stir well. Pour into an 8-by-8-inch baking dish sprayed with butter-flavored cooking spray. Bake 30 minutes or until hot and cheese is melted through.

Hints: 1. 1 1/3 cups uncooked rice usually make about 2 cups cooked.
2. Purchase cooked chicken breast from your local deli and dice it when you get home.

Each serving equals:
HE: 1 3/4 Pr, 1 Ve, 1 Br, 1/2 Fa, 1/2 SM
237 Calories, 6 gm Fa, 20 gm Pr, 25 gm Ca, 211 mg So, 4 Fi
DIABETIC: 2 Mt, 2 St, 1 Ve

Taco Chicken with Vegetables

The aroma that floats from your kitchen while you're preparing this dish is so wonderful, the neighbors may just drop in unexpectedly. Maybe you should double the recipe and be prepared. ☻ Serves 4

> 3 tablespoons taco seasoning ☆
> 16 ounces boned and skinned chicken breasts, cut into 4
>   serving pieces
> 1 cup frozen whole-kernel corn, thawed
> 1½ cups frozen green beans, thawed
> 1½ cups frozen carrot slices, thawed
> ¾ cup chopped onion
> 1¾ cups (one 14½-ounce can) canned Mexican-style stewed
>   tomatoes, undrained

Preheat oven to 350 degrees. Pat 2 tablespoons taco seasoning onto all sides of chicken breast pieces. Place chicken in 8-by-8-inch baking dish sprayed with butter-flavored cooking spray. In a large bowl, combine corn, green beans, carrots, and onion. Stir in stewed tomatoes and remaining 1 tablespoon taco seasoning. Spoon vegetable mixture evenly over chicken. Bake 35 to 45 minutes or until chicken is done. When serving, evenly spoon vegetables over chicken pieces.

Each serving equals:
HE: 3 Pr, 2¾ Ve, ½ Br
228 Calories, 2 gm Fa, 30 gm Pr, 23 gm Ca, 412 mg So, 4 Fi
DIABETIC: 3 Mt, 2 Ve, ½ St

Creamy Chicken Stir Fry

The flavors of the Orient meet the convenience of soup from a can—and "stir fry" will never be the same! This is so fast, and so good, you'll want to serve it all the time. This dish is great served with rice, pasta, or baked potatoes. ●   Serves 4 (1 cup)

> 3½ cups purchased stir-fry vegetables (fresh or frozen)
> ⅓ cup water
> 1 cup (6 ounces) diced cooked chicken breast
> 1 (10¾-ounce) can Campbell's Healthy Request Cream of
>   Chicken Soup
> ¼ teaspoon black pepper

In a large skillet sprayed with butter-flavored cooking spray, sauté vegetables 4 to 5 minutes, stirring often. Add water. Lower heat. Cover and simmer 5 minutes. Stir in chicken, chicken soup, and black pepper. Continue cooking until heated through, stirring occasionally.

Hints: 1. You can use any chopped vegetables of your choice if you don't want to use purchased stir-fry vegetables.
2. Purchase cooked chicken breast at the deli and dice it when you get home.

Each serving equals:

HE: 1¾ Ve, 1½ Pr, ½ Sl, 8 OC

146 Calories, 3 gm Fa, 16 gm Pr, 14 gm Ca, 387 mg So, 2 Fi

DIABETIC: 2 Ve, 1½ Mt

Turkey with Vegetable Sauce

If you want to impress anyone with your culinary skills, this is the dish to do it. Best of all, it's a great way to use up leftover roast turkey—and you can never have enough of those! If there's no leftover turkey, purchase cooked turkey breast from your local deli. ○ Serves 4

1/2 cup chopped onion

1/4 cup chopped green bell pepper

1/2 teaspoon minced garlic

1/2 teaspoon dried thyme leaves

21/4 cups fresh chopped tomatoes

1/2 teaspoon lemon pepper

2 teaspoons Sprinkle Sweet or Sugar Twin

12 ounces baked turkey breast, cut into 4 slices

In a large skillet sprayed with butter-flavored cooking spray, sauté onion, green pepper, and garlic until crisp-tender. Add thyme, tomatoes, lemon pepper, and Sprinkle Sweet. Simmer for 5 minutes. Warm turkey slices in microwave. For each serving, place 1/4 of turkey slices on a plate. Spoon sauce evenly over turkey. Serve at once.

Each serving equals:

HE: 3 Pr, 1½ Ve, 1 OC

147 Calories, 1 gm Fa, 27 gm Pr, 7 gm Ca, 191 mg So, 1 Fi

DIABETIC: 3 Mt, 1 Ve

Party Turkey Tetrazzini

I fell in love with this dish the first time I prepared it—and three years later, it's still one of my favorites. I hope it makes your list of best-loved recipes, too! You can substitute chicken or ham for turkey. ☺ Serves 4

½ cup chopped onion
1½ cups (8 ounces) diced cooked turkey breast
1 (10¾-ounce) can Campbell's Healthy Request Cream of
    Mushroom Soup
¾ cup (3 ounces) Kraft shredded reduced-fat
    Cheddar cheese
2 cups cooked spaghetti
2 tablespoons canned chopped pimiento
2 tablespoons chopped fresh parsley or 1 teaspoon dried
    parsley flakes
⅛ teaspoon black pepper

In a large skillet sprayed with butter-flavored cooking spray, sauté onion and turkey until onion is tender. Blend in mushroom soup and Cheddar cheese. Cook over low heat until cheese is melted, stirring often. Add spaghetti, pimiento, parsley, and black pepper. Continue cooking until heated through.

Hints: 1. 1½ cups uncooked spaghetti usually make about 2 cups cooked.
2. Break the spaghetti into about four-inch pieces before cooking.

Each serving equals:
HE: 3 Pr, 1 Br, ¼ Ve, ½ Sl, 1 OC
271 Calories, 5 gm Fa, 27 gm Pr, 29 gm Ca, 515 mg So, 1 Fi
DIABETIC: 2½ Mt, 2 St

Cheesy Tuna Noodle Bake

I took two of my favorite "comfort dishes" (aren't they yours, too?), threw them together, and came up with a new "comfort dish" that is out of this world. ☻ Serves 6

> 3 cups cooked noodles, rinsed and drained
> 1 cup frozen peas
> 1 tablespoon dried onion flakes
> 1 (10¾-ounce) can Campbell's Healthy Request Cream of
>   Mushroom Soup
> 1 (6-ounce) can tuna, packed in water, drained and flaked
> 1 scant cup (3¾ ounces) Kraft shredded reduced-fat
>   Cheddar cheese
> 1 tablespoon Dijon mustard
> ⅛ teaspoon black pepper

Preheat oven to 350 degrees. In a large bowl, combine noodles, peas, onion flakes, and mushroom soup. Add tuna, Cheddar cheese, mustard, and black pepper. Pour into an 8-by-8-inch baking dish sprayed with butter-flavored cooking spray. Cover and bake 30 minutes. Uncover and bake an additional 5 minutes.

Hint: 2⅔ cups uncooked noodles usually make 3 cups cooked.

Each serving equals:
HE: 1⅓ Pr, 1⅓ Br, ¼ Sl, 8 OC
231 Calories, 5 gm Fa, 18 gm Pr, 28 gm Ca, 540 mg So, 2 Fi
DIABETIC: 1½ Mt, 1½ St

Cajun Fish

Once you try fish baked this way, I don't think you'll ever be satisfied with plain broiled fish again. The Cajun stewed tomatoes really do the trick. Maybe food like this is why those folks in New Orleans always feel like dancing. ○   Serves 4

> 16 ounces white fish (orange roughy, sole, or flounder), cut
>   into 8 pieces
> 6 tablespoons (1½ ounces) fine dried bread crumbs
> ¼ cup finely chopped onion
> 1 tablespoon + 1 teaspoon reduced-calorie margarine
> 1¾ cups (one 14½-ounce can) canned Cajun-style stewed
>   tomatoes, with juice

Preheat oven to 350 degrees. Rinse fish in cold water. Pat dry. Spray an 8-by-8-inch baking dish with butter-flavored cooking spray. Place fish in dish. Sprinkle bread crumbs and onions evenly over fish. Dot with margarine. Bake for 20 minutes. Pour stewed tomatoes over fish and continue to bake 20 minutes longer.

Hint: Regular canned stewed tomatoes and 1 teaspoon Cajun seasoning can be used in place of Cajun-style stewed tomatoes.

Each serving equals:
   HE: 1½ Pr, 1 Ve, ½ Br, ½ Fa
   185 Calories, 3 gm Fa, 24 gm Pr, 15 gm Ca, 515 mg So, 1 Fi
   DIABETIC: 3 Mt, ½ Ve, ½ St

Stuffed Baked Fish

This easy fish dish made a big hit with Cliff, who's always been kind of "so-so" when it came to eating fish. Now he's willing to try new fish dishes on a regular basis—and I have this recipe to thank for changing his mind. ☻ Serves 4

½ cup chopped onion
4 slices reduced-calorie white bread, crumbled
1 teaspoon dried basil leaves
⅛ teaspoon black pepper
4 (2-ounce) white fish fillets
2 teaspoons reduced-calorie margarine
½ teaspoon paprika

Preheat oven to 400 degrees. In a large skillet sprayed with butter-flavored cooking spray, sauté onions until tender. Add bread crumbs, basil, and black pepper. Mix well. Layer stuffing mixture evenly in an 8-by-8-inch baking dish sprayed with butter-flavored cooking spray. Place fillets on top of stuffing. Melt margarine and drizzle over fish. Sprinkle paprika on top. Bake 15 to 20 minutes or until fish flakes easily.

Hint: Use day-old or slightly dried bread. It makes good crumbs.

Each serving equals:

HE: ¾ Pr, ½ Br, ¼ Fa, ¼ Ve
103 Calories, 1 gm Fa, 14 gm Pr, 9 gm Ca, 145 mg So, 1 Fi
DIABETIC: 1½ Mt, ½ St

Salmon-Vegetable Casserole

My son Tommy thought this dish was very "uptown" in flavor. He asks me to prepare it at least once a month. When you can please "growing boys" with a fish dish, you know you did something right. ● Serves 4

1 (10¾-ounce) can Campbell's Healthy Request Cream of
  Mushroom Soup
1 cup skim milk
1⅓ cups (4 ounces) uncooked instant rice
½ cup (4 ounces) Philadelphia fat-free cream cheese
6 ounces canned salmon, flaked and boned
2 cups (one 16-ounce can) green beans, rinsed and drained
2 cups (one 16-ounce can) carrots, rinsed and drained
1 tablespoon dried onion flakes
2 tablespoons canned chopped pimiento
⅓ cup (1 ounce) canned French-fried onion rings

Preheat oven to 350 degrees. In a medium saucepan, combine mushroom soup and milk. Heat until warm. Add rice. Cover and let stand 5 minutes. Add cream cheese, salmon, green beans, carrots, dried onion flakes, and pimiento. Mix well to combine. Spray an 8-by-8-inch baking dish with butter-flavored cooking spray. Pour mixture into dish. Bake covered 30 minutes. Top with onion rings and continue baking uncovered for an additional 10 minutes.

Each serving equals:

HE: 2 Ve, 2 Pr, 1 Br, ¼ SM, ½ Sl, 9 OC
327 Calories, 7 gm Fa, 20 gm Pr, 46 gm Ca, 1,013 mg So, 3 Fi
DIABETIC: 2 Ve, 2 Pr, 2 St

Pork Cutlets with Corn Stuffing

This dish made a believer out of my son James, convincing him that healthy could still be tasty. He remarked at least twice, while relishing every bite, "Are you sure this is diet food? It just doesn't taste like it." ◐ Serves 4

4 (3-ounce) lean pork cutlets or tenderloins
1/4 cup chopped onion
1/4 cup chopped green bell pepper
2 cups (one 16-ounce can) cream-style corn
1 egg, beaten, or equivalent in egg substitute
2 slices reduced-calorie bread, crumbled
1/8 teaspoon black pepper

Preheat oven to 350 degrees. In a large skillet sprayed with butter-flavored cooking spray, brown cutlets. Place browned cutlets in an 8-by-8-inch baking dish. In a medium bowl, combine onion, green pepper, corn, egg, bread, and black pepper. Mix well to combine. Place corn stuffing mixture on top of cutlets. Cover. Bake 1 hour.

Hint: Don't overbrown cutlets, or meat will turn out tough.

Each serving equals:
HE: 2½ Pr (¼ limited), 1¼ Br, ¼ Ve
278 Calories, 8 gm Fa, 24 gm Pr, 28 gm Ca, 466 mg So, 2 Fi
DIABETIC: 2½ Mt, 2 St

Pork Cutlets Creole

There's just enough Creole flavor in this recipe without being overpowering. This is definitely for people who like to live on the spicier side of the street—but not all the way down the block!

○   Serves 4

> 4 (3-ounce) lean pork cutlets or tenderloins
> ⅛ teaspoon black pepper
> 4 slices onion
> 4 rings green bell pepper
> 1¾ cups (one 15-ounce can) Hunt's Chunky Tomato Sauce
> ⅛ teaspoon thyme
> ¼ cup water
> 1 teaspoon Brown Sugar Twin
> ½ cup cooked rice

Preheat oven to 350 degrees. In a skillet sprayed with butter-flavored cooking spray, brown cutlets. Place browned cutlets in an 8-by-8-inch baking dish. Sprinkle each cutlet with black pepper. Top each with an onion slice and a green pepper ring. In a medium bowl, combine tomato sauce, thyme, water, Brown Sugar Twin, and cooked rice. Pour mixture over cutlets. Cover. Bake 30 minutes.

Hint: ⅓ cup uncooked rice usually makes about ½ cup cooked.

Each serving equals:

HE: 2¼ Pr, 2 Ve, ¼ Br, 1 OC

247 Calories, 8 gm Fa, 21 gm Pr, 23 gm Ca, 647 mg So, 2 Fi

DIABETIC: 2½ Mt, 2 Ve, ½ St

Yankee Noodle Bake

This recipe is about as all-American as you can get with "throw-together" ingredients. The slight barbecue flavor comes through loud and clear. ☻ Serves 4

8 ounces (½ package) sliced Healthy Choice 97% fat-free
    frankfurters
½ cup chopped green bell pepper
½ cup chopped onion
2 cups cooked noodles, rinsed and drained
1¾ cups (one 15-ounce can) Hunt's Chunky Tomato Sauce
1 tablespoon Brown Sugar Twin
1 teaspoon prepared mustard
⅛ teaspoon black pepper

Preheat oven to 350 degrees. In a skillet sprayed with butter-flavored cooking spray, brown frankfurters, green pepper, and onion. Add noodles, tomato sauce, Brown Sugar Twin, mustard, and black pepper. Mix well to combine. Pour into an 8-by-8-inch baking dish. Bake 30 minutes.

Hint: A full 1¾ cups uncooked noodles usually make about 2
    cups cooked.

Each serving equals:
    HE: 2¼ Ve, 1⅓ Pr, 1 Br, 1 OC
    226 Calories, 4 gm Fa, 13 gm Pr, 35 gm Ca, 1,203 mg So, 3 Fi
    DIABETIC: 2 Ve, 1 Mt, 1 St

Potato and Sausage Salad

Yes, this is a potato salad, but it's so substantial in flavor and texture that it deserves to be the main attraction instead of just a side dish. The caraway seeds make it extra tangy.

● Serves 6 (¾ cup)

3 full cups (16 ounces) diced cooked potatoes
2 tablespoons cider vinegar
¼ cup chopped onions or 4 chopped green onions
½ cup Kraft fat-free mayonnaise
2 teaspoons prepared horseradish
⅛ teaspoon black pepper
1 teaspoon caraway seeds
6 ounces Healthy Choice 97% fat-free kielbasa sausage,
*   cooked, cooled, and sliced*
4 (¾-ounce) slices Weight Watchers reduced-fat Swiss
*   cheese, shredded*

Place sliced potatoes in a large bowl. Gently mix in vinegar and onions. In a small bowl, combine mayonnaise, horseradish, black pepper, and caraway seeds. Add to potatoes. Stir in sausage and Swiss cheese. Mix gently to combine. Refrigerate for at least 1 hour.

Hint: If you can't find Healthy Choice kielbasa, use Healthy Choice frankfurters.

Each serving equals:

HE: 1⅓ Pr, ⅔ Br, 13 OC
162 Calories, 4 gm Fa, 9 gm Pr, 23 gm Ca, 622 mg So, 1 Fi
DIABETIC: 1 Mt, 1 St

Sausage and Sauerkraut Casserole

My Bohemian heritage shines through in this savory dish. My Grandma Nowachek would be proud that I prepared her traditional dish in an untraditional way—and kept the flavor intact. ● Serves 4

> 8 ounces Healthy Choice 97% fat-free kielbasa sausage, cooked, cooled, and sliced
> 2 cups cooked noodles, rinsed and drained
> 2 cups (one 16-ounce can) sauerkraut, well drained
> 1 (10¾-ounce) can Campbell's Healthy Request Cream of Mushroom Soup
> 1 teaspoon caraway seeds
> ⅛ teaspoon black pepper

Preheat oven to 350 degrees. In a medium bowl, combine sausage, noodles, and sauerkraut. Add mushroom soup, caraway seeds, and black pepper. Mix well to combine. Pour into an 8-by-8-inch baking dish sprayed with cooking spray. Cover. Bake 45 minutes. Uncover and bake an additional 15 minutes.

Hints: 1. You can substitute Healthy Choice frankfurters for the sausage.
2. A full 1¾ cups uncooked noodles usually make about 2 cups cooked.

Each serving equals:

HE: 1⅓ Pr, 1 Br, 1 Ve, ½ Sl, 4 OC
247 Calories, 5 gm Fa, 16 gm Pr, 35 gm Ca, 1,562 mg So, 3 Fi
DIABETIC: 1½ Mt, 1½ St, 1 Ve

Red Flannel Hash

If you've never thought of including beets in a hash before, I think you will be pleasantly surprised by how much color, flavor, and texture they add to what otherwise would be a real "leftovers" dish. Now my hash doesn't taste like "rehashed" food anymore.

☉   Serves 4

> ½ cup finely chopped onion
>
> 3 full cups (10 ounces) frozen shredded potatoes, thawed, or
>   raw shredded potatoes
>
> 2 cups (one 16-ounce can) canned beets, rinsed, drained,
>   and finely chopped
>
> Two 2.5-ounce packages finely chopped Carl Buddig 90%
>   lean corned beef
>
> ⅛ teaspoon black pepper
>
> ⅓ cup Carnation nonfat dry milk powder
>
> ½ cup water
>
> 1 tablespoon + 1 teaspoon reduced-calorie margarine

In a large heavy-bottomed skillet sprayed with butter-flavored cooking spray, sauté onion until tender. In a large bowl combine cooked onion, potatoes, beets, corned beef, and black pepper. In a small bowl, combine dry milk powder and water. Add to potato mixture. Mix gently until well blended. Melt margarine in same skillet. Spread hash mixture evenly in skillet. Cook over medium heat until browned.

Each serving equals:

HE: 1¼ Pr, 1¼ Ve, ½ Br, ½ Fa, ¼ SM

175 Calories, 4 gm Fa, 11 gm Pr, 24 gm Ca, 792 mg So, 3 Fi

DIABETIC: 1 Mt, 1 Ve, 1 St

Reuben Casserole

If Reuben sandwiches are among your favorites, this flavorful casserole was created with you in mind. Cliff loved it—really loved it. He says that it's hard work being the "official taste-tester," but dishes like this are worth all the work he puts in fulfilling his obligations. ● Serves 4

1/4 cup Kraft fat-free mayonnaise
1/4 cup Kraft fat-free Thousand Island dressing
2 cups (one 16-ounce can) sauerkraut, well drained
One 2.5-ounce package sliced Carl Buddig 90% lean corned beef
4 (3/4 ounce) slices (3/4 cup) Weight Watchers reduced-fat Swiss cheese, shredded
1 cup sliced fresh tomato
2 slices reduced-calorie rye bread, cut into small pieces

Preheat oven to 350 degrees. In a small bowl, combine mayonnaise and Thousand Island dressing. Layering in an 8-by-8-inch baking dish, place sauerkraut on bottom, then corned beef, dressing mixture, Swiss cheese, and tomatoes. In a nonstick pan sprayed with butter-flavored cooking spray, lightly sauté bread. Sprinkle on top of tomatoes. Bake 20 minutes.

Each serving equals:

HE: 1²/₃ Pr, 1½ Ve, ¼ Br, ¼ Sl, 8 OC
189 Calories, 7 gm Fa, 11 gm Pr, 21 gm Ca, 1,663 mg So, 2 Fi
DIABETIC: 1½ Mt, 1 Ve, 1 St

Cabbage-Ham Quiche

This combination has to be tried to be believed—the ham, cabbage, and Swiss cheese blend so well, you're bound to declare this one a winner! ● Serves 8

1 Pillsbury refrigerated unbaked 9-inch piecrust
1 full cup (6 ounces) diced Dubuque 97% fat-free or any
    extra-lean ham
1/2 cup chopped onion
3 1/2 cups chopped cabbage
1 cup hot water
2/3 cup Carnation nonfat dry milk powder
1 cup cold water
2 eggs, slightly beaten, or equivalent in egg substitute
4 (3/4-ounce) slices Weight Watchers reduced-fat Swiss
    cheese, shredded
1/8 teaspoon black pepper
1/2 teaspoon caraway seeds

Bake piecrust according to package directions until *almost* done. Remove from oven. Lower heat to 375 degrees. Sauté ham and onion in a skillet sprayed with butter-flavored cooking spray until onion is tender, about 5 minutes. Add cabbage and hot water. Continue cooking until liquid evaporates and cabbage is golden brown, about 12 minutes. Remove from heat. In a small bowl, combine dry milk powder, cold water, eggs, Swiss cheese, black pepper, and caraway seeds. Stir into cabbage mixture. Pour into partially baked crust. Bake until filling puffs and starts to brown, about 40 minutes.

Each serving equals:
    HE: 1 1/4 Pr (1/4 limited), 1 Ve, 1/2 Br, 1/4 SM, 1/2 Sl, 10 OC
    233 Calories, 12 gm Fa, 11 gm Pr, 20 gm Ca, 538 mg So, 2 Fi
    DIABETIC: 1 Mt, 1 Ve, 1 St, 1 Fa

Ham and Green Bean Casserole

If you don't manage to have this one on the table ready to serve in less than 10 minutes, we might have to call in an efficiency expert. Fast food from the microwave at its tastiest—and healthiest! ☻ Serves 4

> 1 (10³/₄-ounce) can Campbell's Healthy Request Cream of
> Mushroom Soup
> 4 cups (two 16-ounce cans) canned green beans, rinsed
> and drained
> 1 full cup (6 ounces) diced Dubuque 97% fat-free or any
> extra-lean ham
> ⅛ teaspoon black pepper
> ³/₄ cup (3 ounces) Kraft shredded reduced-fat
> Cheddar cheese

In a large bowl, combine mushroom soup, beans, ham, and black pepper. Pour into an 8-by-8-inch microwave-safe baking dish sprayed with butter-flavored cooking spray. Microwave for 6 minutes on HIGH or until hot. Sprinkle Cheddar cheese over top. Microwave 2 minutes more or until cheese melts.

Hint: You can bake this casserole in conventional oven at 350° for 30 minutes.

Each serving equals:
> HE: 2 Pr, 2 Ve, ½ Sl, 1 OC
> 168 Calories, 6 gm Fa, 15 gm Pr, 14 gm Ca, 1,179 mg So, 1 Fi
> DIABETIC: 2 Mt, 2 Ve

Hawaiian Brunch Casserole

If it's ten degrees below zero and the ground's covered with snow, play some island music and see if you don't find it easy to believe you're on vacation! You and your family will relish this delicious casserole that says *aloha* any time of the day—or year.

● Serves 4

> 1 cup (one 8-ounce can) canned crushed pineapple, packed
>   in its own juice, drained (reserve liquid)
> ³/₄ cup Bisquick reduced-fat baking mix
> ²/₃ cup Carnation nonfat dry milk powder
> 2 eggs, slightly beaten, or equivalent in egg substitute
> 2 teaspoons reduced-calorie margarine, melted
> 1 teaspoon Dijon mustard
> ¹/₂ teaspoon onion powder or dried onion flakes
> ¹/₂ cup (3 ounces) diced Dubuque 97% fat-free or any extra-
>   lean ham
> ³/₄ cup (3 ounces) Kraft shredded reduced-fat
>   Cheddar cheese
> 1 finely chopped green onion

Preheat oven to 350 degrees. Add enough water to reserved pineapple juice to make ³/₄ cup liquid. Combine pineapple liquid, baking mix, dry milk powder, eggs, margarine, mustard, and onion powder in blender. Process on BLEND 45 seconds. Pour into medium bowl. Stir in ham, Cheddar cheese, green onion, and pineapple. Pour into an 8-by-8-inch baking dish sprayed with butter-flavored cooking spray. Bake 25 to 30 minutes.

Each serving equals:

   HE: 2 Pr (¹/₂ limited), 1 Br, ¹/₂ SM, ¹/₂ Fr, ¹/₄ Fa
   283 Calories, 9 gm Fa, 19 gm Pr, 32 gm Ca, 727 mg So, 1 Fi
   DIABETIC: 2 Mt, 1 St, ¹/₂ SM, ¹/₂ Fr

Denver Pizza

Who said that a "Denver sandwich" had to be a traditional sandwich? After trying this filling pizza, you may never want the "real thing" again! Trust me when I say to spread the mustard over the crust. You'll be so glad you did.

● Serves 8 (2 pieces each)

1 (11-ounce) can Pillsbury Crusty French Loaf
2 tablespoons prepared mustard
2 full cups (12 ounces) finely diced Dubuque 97% fat-free or
   any extra-lean ham
½ cup chopped onion
¾ cup chopped green bell pepper
1 cup diced fresh tomato
1¼ cups chopped fresh mushrooms
1½ cups (6 ounces) Kraft shredded reduced-fat
   mozzarella cheese
2 teaspoons dried parsley flakes

Preheat oven to 375 degrees. Unroll French Loaf and pat dough into an 11-by-16-inch jelly-roll pan and up sides to form a rim. Bake 8 to 9 minutes. Remove from oven. Spread mustard evenly over crust using a rubber spatula or stiff pastry brush. Layer ham, onion, green pepper, tomato, and mushrooms over crust. Sprinkle cheese and parsley flakes evenly over top. Bake 20 minutes or until cheese is bubbly. Cool 4 to 5 minutes before cutting. Cut into 16 pieces.

Each serving equals:
HE: 2 Pr, 1 Br, 1 Ve
189 Calories, 5 gm Fa, 18 gm Pr, 18 gm Ca, 852 mg So, 2 Fi
DIABETIC: 2 Mt, 1 St

Desserts

I enjoy a juicy apple or ripe peach as much as the next person, but if you told me that fresh fruit was the only kind of dessert I could have for the rest of my life in order to eat healthy, I think I'd drown my depression in a box of cake donuts! Happily, of course, it's not true, and I think I've made the most "converts" to Healthy Exchanges® with the desserts I've created. I always say that it was only when I realized that I needed to enjoy a real dessert every day that I finally gave up dieting for keeps—and found my way to a lifetime of good health and good food through Healthy Exchanges®. The pies, cakes, and other treats in this section offer a delicious abundance of choices—and they don't taste like diet food. You'll get chocolate chips and nuts, creamy cheesecakes, and pies that will make your mouth water. Isn't it wonderful that we can make these treats without the extra sugar and fat, and finally stop feeling deprived? Enjoy!

Baked Apples

Have you ever noticed that when you reach for a plain apple to chase away hunger pangs, you wind up hungrier after you've finished munching? I think it's because your taste buds have just started to have fun—and then the party's over. But take that same small apple, baked in this easy way, and this satisfies in a way that plain apple just never does. I think it's the combination of warmth and softness that does the trick. ☉   Serves 4

> 4 small Rome Beauty apples
> 4 tablespoons raisins
> 1/4 cup (1 ounce) chopped walnuts
> 1 tablespoon + 1 teaspoon reduced-calorie margarine,
>   melted
> 1 tablespoon Brown Sugar Twin
> 1/4 cup lemon juice
> 1/4 cup water
> 1 teaspoon apple-pie spice

Preheat oven to 350 degrees. Pare apple skin 1/3 of the way down from tops of apples. Core and slice apples, leaving bottoms attached. Place apples in an 8-by-8-inch baking dish. In a small bowl, combine raisins, walnuts, margarine, and Brown Sugar Twin. Stuff mixture in the center of the apples. In a small bowl, combine lemon juice, water, and apple-pie spice. Pour over and around apples. Bake 30 to 40 minutes, uncovered, or until apples are tender, basting every 10 minutes.

Each serving equals:
HE: 1 1/2 Fr, 1 Fa, 1/4 Pr, 2 OC
141 Calories, 6 gm Fa, 1 gm Pr, 21 gm Ca, 23 mg So, 2 Fi
DIABETIC: 1 1/2 Fr, 1 Fa

Cherry Crunch

Munch away on this crunchy cherry treat whenever you like. My kids James and Pam do on a regular basis and enjoy every bite. I hope my grandkids love it as much when they are old enough to join the "Taste-Testing Team." ● Serves 6

1 cup (3 ounces) quick oats
6 tablespoons flour
3 tablespoons Brown Sugar Twin
¼ cup reduced-calorie margarine, melted
3 cups pitted fresh red cherries
1½ cups water
1 (4-serving) package Jell-O sugar-free cherry gelatin
1 (4-serving) package Jell-O sugar-free vanilla cook-and-
  serve pudding mix
¼ teaspoon almond extract

Preheat oven to 350 degrees. In a medium bowl, combine oats, flour, and Brown Sugar Twin until well blended. Add melted margarine. Mix until crumbly. Spray an 8-by-8-inch baking dish with butter-flavored cooking spray. Spread half the crumb mixture on bottom of dish. Place drained cherries on top of crumbs. In a medium saucepan, combine water, dry gelatin, and dry pudding mix. Cook to boiling, stirring constantly. Remove from heat. Stir in almond extract. Pour hot mixture over cherries. Top with remaining half of crumbs. Bake 45 minutes. Cool on wire rack.

Hints: 1. Try this crunch with 1 tablespoon Cool Whip Lite, but don't forget to count the few additional calories.
2. Frozen cherries, thawed and drained, or two 16-ounce cans, packed in water and drained, can be used in place of fresh cherries.

Each serving equals:
HE: 1 Fr, 1 Br, 1 Fa, ¼ Sl, 1 OC
171 Calories, 3 gm Fa, 5 gm Pr, 31 gm Ca, 175 mg So, 1 Fi
DIABETIC: 1 Fr, 1 St, ½ Fa

Rhubarb Crunch

I love rhubarb—and I love foods that crunch. One of my favorite memories of springtime when I was young is of my mother stirring up a rhubarb crunch—and my getting to eat a piece of it warm from the oven. That's how I feel all over again when I enjoy a piece of this treat now. ☻   Serves 6

1 cup (3 ounces) quick oats

6 tablespoons flour

1 teaspoon cinnamon

3 tablespoons Brown Sugar Twin

¼ cup reduced-calorie margarine, melted

4 cups diced rhubarb

1 (4-serving) package Jell-O sugar-free strawberry gelatin

1 (4-serving) package Jell-O sugar-free vanilla cook-and-serve pudding mix

1½ cups water

1 teaspoon vanilla extract

Preheat oven to 350 degrees. In a medium bowl, combine oats, flour, cinnamon, and Brown Sugar Twin until well blended. Add melted margarine. Mix until crumbly. Set aside. Place rhubarb in an 8-by-8-inch baking dish. In a medium saucepan, combine dry gelatin, dry pudding mix, and water. Cook to boiling, stirring constantly. Remove from heat. Stir in vanilla extract. Pour hot mixture over diced rhubarb. Top with crumbs. Bake 1 hour. Cool on a wire rack.

Hint: 1 tablespoon Cool Whip Lite is a great topping for this dessert, but don't forget to count the few additional calories.

Each serving equals:

HE: 1⅓ Ve, 1 Br, 1 Fa, ¼ SI, 2 OC

142 Calories, 3 gm Fa, 5 gm Pr, 23 gm Ca, 170 mg So, 2 Fi

DIABETIC: 1 St, 1 Fa, 1 Free Food

Cinnamon Peach Bread Pudding

When I first removed this from the microwave and spooned up a dish for my son Tommy, I didn't know what he'd think of it because he's not really crazy about raisins. But after one bite, he sure had a big smile on his face. In fact, he remarked that maybe he should give those "brown things" another chance!

○ Serves 4

8 slices reduced-calorie white
   bread
1 tablespoon + 1 teaspoon
   reduced-calorie margarine
2 tablespoons peach spreadable
   fruit spread
1⅓ cups skim milk

2 eggs or equivalent in egg
   substitute
2 tablespoons Sprinkle Sweet or
   Sugar Twin
½ teaspoon cinnamon
1 teaspoon vanilla extract
2 tablespoons raisins

Toast bread. Spread with margarine and peach spreadable fruit. Cube bread. Pour skim milk into 4-cup glass measure. Scald, but *do not boil milk* in microwave about 4 to 7 minutes on HIGH. Let cool. In a large bowl, stir eggs with wire whisk. Add Sprinkle Sweet, cinnamon, and vanilla extract. Stir in scalded milk. Mix well to combine. Add bread and raisins. Mix well. Let set about 10 minutes for bread to absorb milk. Pour into an 8-by-8-inch microwave-safe baking dish. Bake at 50% or MEDIUM power in microwave for about 10 minutes. Spoon into 4 dessert dishes.

Hint: You can top this with 1 tablespoon Cool Whip Lite, but count additional calories accordingly.

Each serving equals:

HE: 1 Br, ¾ Fr, ½ Fa, ½ Pr (limited), ⅓ SM, 2 OC
197 Calories, 4 gm Fa, 12 gm Pr, 29 gm Ca, 280 mg So, 2 Fi
DIABETIC: 1 St, 1 Mt, 1 Fr

Mandarin Rice Pudding

You may never have imagined this flavor combination when you thought of rice pudding, but after trying it, I'll bet you will in the future. The mandarin oranges and banana-pudding mix are just perfect with the rice and cinnamon. ○ Serves 6

> 1 (4-serving) package Jell-O sugar-free banana instant-
>   pudding mix
> ⅔ cup Carnation nonfat dry milk powder
> 1½ cups water
> 1 teaspoon vanilla extract
> 1 teaspoon cinnamon
> ¼ cup Cool Whip Lite
> 1½ cups cooked rice
> ½ cup raisins
> 1 cup (one 11-ounce can) canned mandarin oranges, rinsed
>   and drained

In a large bowl combine dry pudding mix, dry milk powder, and water. Mix well using a wire whisk. Blend in vanilla extract, cinnamon, and Cool Whip Lite. Add rice, raisins, and mandarin oranges. Mix gently to combine. Spoon mixture evenly into 6 dessert dishes. Refrigerate for at least 30 minutes.

Hints: 1. 1 cup uncooked rice makes 1½ cups cooked rice.
2. To plump up raisins without "cooking," place in glass measuring cup and microwave on HIGH for 30 seconds.

Each serving equals:
HE: 1 Fr, ½ Br, ⅓ SM, ¼ Sl, 2 OC
142 Calories, less than 1 gm Fa, 4 gm Pr, 31 gm Ca, 266 mg So, 2 Fi
DIABETIC: 1 Fr, 1 St

Fruit Pizza

Cliff knows this page number in my cookbook *by heart*. He tells everyone he knows to give this recipe a try. It's one of his favorite desserts—and one of mine, too. If strawberries and blueberries aren't in season, just let your imagination go wild with whatever fruits *you choose* to include.

● Serves 8 (1 square or 4 bars)

1 (8-ounce) can Pillsbury refrigerated crescent rolls

1 (8-ounce) package Philadelphia fat-free cream cheese

1 teaspoon vanilla extract

Sugar substitute to equal 2 teaspoons sugar

2 cups (two 8-ounce cans) canned crushed pineapple, packed in its own juice, well drained

2 cups fresh strawberries, sliced

1½ cups blueberries, fresh or frozen, thawed and drained

1 (4-serving) package Jell-O sugar-free mixed fruit gelatin

1 (4-serving) package Jell-O sugar-free vanilla cook-and-serve pudding mix

1½ cups water

Preheat oven to 425 degrees. Spray medium-size pizza pan or cookie sheet with butter-flavored cooking spray. Pat rolls in pan, being sure to seal perforations. Bake 7 to 8 minutes or until lightly browned. Cool on wire rack. In a medium bowl, stir cream cheese with spoon until soft. Blend in vanilla extract and sugar substitute. Spread mixture evenly over cooled crust. Layer pineapple over cream-cheese mixture. Sprinkle strawberries and blueberries over pineapple. In a medium saucepan, combine dry gelatin, dry pudding mix, and water. Cook over medium heat until mixture comes to a boil, stirring constantly. Spoon hot mixture evenly over fruit until entire pan is covered with glaze. Refrigerate

for at least 2 hours before serving. Cut into 8 squares or 32 bars.
Refrigerate leftovers.

Hint: Do not use inexpensive crescent rolls. They will not cover
the pan properly.

Each serving equals:

HE: 1 Br, 1 Fr, ½ Pr, 15 OC

204 Calories, 6 gm Fa, 7 gm Pr, 31 gm Ca, 501 mg So, 2 Fi

DIABETIC: 1 St, 1 Fr, 1 Fa

Hawaiian Fruit Squares

These pineapple treats are anything but "square"! After a few bites, you could close your eyes and feel as if you are lounging under a palm tree on the Big Island without a care in the world.

❂   Serves 8 (1 square or 4 bars)

> 1 (8-ounce) can Pillsbury refrigerated crescent rolls
> 1 (8-ounce) package Philadelphia fat-free cream cheese
> 2 tablespoons Sprinkle Sweet or Sugar Twin
> 1 tablespoon lemon juice
> 1 teaspoon coconut extract
> 2 eggs or equivalent in egg substitute
> 3 tablespoons flaked coconut
> 1 cup (one 8-ounce can) canned crushed pineapple, packed
>   in its own juice, well drained

Preheat oven to 375 degrees. Spray a 9-by-13-inch rimmed cookie sheet with butter-flavored cooking spray. Pat rolls in pan, being sure to seal perforations. Bake 5 minutes. Remove from oven. In a medium bowl, stir cream cheese with a spoon until soft. Add Sprinkle Sweet, lemon juice, coconut extract, and eggs. Blend until smooth. Stir in coconut and pineapple. Mix well. Spread mixture evenly over partially baked crust. Bake an additional 20 to 25 minutes, or until crust is golden brown and filling is set. Cool completely on wire rack. Cut into 8 squares or 32 bars. Refrigerate leftovers.

Hint: Do not use inexpensive crescent rolls. They will not cover the pan properly.

Each serving equals:

HE: 1 Br, ¾ Pr (¼ limited), ¼ Fr, 7 OC

175 Calories, 8 gm Fa, 8 gm Pr, 18 gm Ca, 422 mg So, 1 Fi

DIABETIC: 1 St, 1 Mt, 1 Fa

Judy's Chocolate Toffee Crescent Bars

These tasty "cookies" may be prepared with a bread product, but I promise you, once these are finished baking, you won't be thinking of sandwiches. ● Serves 16 (2 bars)

1 (8-ounce) can Pillsbury refrigerated crescent rolls
¼ cup Brown Sugar Twin
⅓ cup reduced-calorie margarine
½ cup (2 ounces) chopped walnuts
⅔ cup (4 ounces) mini chocolate chips

Preheat oven to 350 degrees. Pat rolls into an ungreased 10-by-15-inch jelly-roll pan. Gently press dough to cover bottom of pan, being sure to seal perforations. In a small saucepan, combine Brown Sugar Twin and margarine. Boil 1 minute. Pour mixture evenly over dough. Sprinkle with walnuts. Bake 12 to 16 minutes or until golden brown. Remove from oven and immediately sprinkle with chocolate chips. Slightly swirl pieces as they melt, leaving some pieces partially whole to create an uneven appearance. Cool on wire rack. Cut into 32 bars.

Hint: Do not use inexpensive crescent rolls. They will not cover the pan properly.

Each serving equals:

HE: ¾ Fa, ½ Br, ½ Sl, 7 OC

122 Calories, 8 gm Fa, 2 gm Pr, 11 gm Ca, 135 mg So, 1 Fi

DIABETIC: 1 Fa, 1 St

Carrot Cake
with Cream-Cheese Topping

You'll notice that I use canned carrots in this recipe. Because the baking process is much shorter for baked goods without excess fat, fresh carrots just don't work as well. But my version still has all the great taste of a carrot cake—and the creamy topping that tastes just right with it. ✿ Serves 8

2 tablespoons vegetable oil
1 cup unsweetened applesauce
3 tablespoons Brown Sugar Twin
¼ cup Sprinkle Sweet ☆
2 eggs, well beaten, or equivalent in egg substitute
1 cup (one 8-ounce can) canned carrots, drained, rinsed, and diced
¼ cup water
1½ cups cake flour
½ teaspoon salt
½ teaspoon baking powder
½ teaspoon baking soda
½ teaspoon cinnamon
2 teaspoons vanilla extract ☆
¼ cup (1 ounce) chopped walnuts ☆
¼ cup raisins
1 (8-ounce) package Philadelphia fat-free cream cheese
Sugar substitute to equal 1 tablespoon sugar
½ cup Cool Whip Lite

Preheat oven to 350 degrees. In a large bowl, combine vegetable oil, applesauce, Brown Sugar Twin, and all but 1 tablespoon Sprinkle Sweet. Add eggs, carrots, and water. Mix just to combine. In a medium-sized bowl, combine cake flour, salt, baking powder, baking soda, and cinnamon. Stir cake-flour mixture into carrot mixture. Add 1 teaspoon vanilla extract, 2 tablespoons walnuts, and raisins. Mix gently to combine. Pour batter into an 8-by-8-inch baking dish sprayed with butter-flavored cooking spray. Bake 30 minutes or until toothpick inserted in center comes out clean. Cool on wire rack. In a medium bowl, stir cream cheese with a spoon until soft. Add remaining 1 tablespoon Sprinkle Sweet, remaining 1 teaspoon vanilla extract, and Cool Whip Lite. Mix gently to combine. Spread mixture evenly over cooled cake. Sprinkle remaining 2 tablespoons walnuts evenly over top. (Refrigerate leftovers.)

Each serving equals:

HE: 1 Fa, 1 Br, ¾ Pr (¼ limited), ½ Fr, ¼ Ve, ¼ Sl

215 Calories, 10 gm Fa, 7 gm Pr, 24 gm Ca, 504 mg So, 3 Fi

DIABETIC: 2 Fa, 1 St, 1 Fr

Pineapple Cake

This rich, moist cake should fill your day with sunshine, even if it's snowing or pouring rain outside. Pineapple is so full of natural sweetness, it makes a terrific dessert with almost no added sweetener. ○ Serves 8

2 tablespoons vegetable oil
½ cup unsweetened applesauce
3 tablespoons Brown Sugar
  Twin
3 tablespoons Sprinkle Sweet or
  Sugar Twin
2 eggs, beaten, or equivalent in
  egg substitute
2 tablespoons raisins

2 cups (two 8-ounce cans)
  canned crushed pineapple,
  packed in its own juice, well
  drained (reserve liquid)
1½ cups cake flour
½ teaspoon salt
½ teaspoon baking powder
½ teaspoon baking soda
1 teaspoon vanilla extract

Preheat oven to 350 degrees. In a large bowl, combine vegetable oil, applesauce, Brown Sugar Twin, and Sprinkle Sweet. Add eggs, raisins, and crushed pineapple. Add enough water to reserved pineapple juice to make ½ cup liquid. Add liquid to applesauce mixture. Mix just to combine. In a medium bowl, combine flour, salt, baking powder, and baking soda. Stir into pineapple mixture. Add vanilla extract. Mix to combine. Pour batter into an 8-by-8-inch baking dish sprayed with butter-flavored cooking spray. Bake 30 minutes or until cake tests done. Cool on wire rack.

Hint: This cake is good served with a tablespoon of Cool Whip Lite, but don't forget to count the few additional calories.

Each serving equals:

HE: 1 Br, ¾ Fa, ¾ Fr, ¼ Pr (limited), 5 OC

177 Calories, 7 gm Fa, 3 gm Pr, 26 gm Ca, 290 mg So, 2 Fi

DIABETIC: 1 St, 1 Fa, 1 Fr

Black Forest Pie

I created this one while riding my bike home wondering what I was going to do with all the ripe cherries in my backyard. I quickly picked a few, threw this together, and ever since have been "coming up cherries" every time I serve this "cherry pie" to anyone. Now that's what I call hitting the jackpot! ⊙   Serves 8

1½ cups water
1 (4-serving) package Jell-O sugar-free cherry gelatin
1 (4-serving) package Jell-O sugar-free vanilla cook-and-
    serve pudding mix
2 cups pitted red cherries, fresh, frozen, or canned, packed
    in water, drained
½ teaspoon almond extract
1 (6-ounce) Keebler chocolate-flavored piecrust
1 (8-ounce) package Philadelphia fat-free cream cheese
¼ cup Cool Whip Lite
1 teaspoon vanilla extract
Sugar substitute to equal 2 teaspoons sugar
¼ cup (1 ounce) chopped walnuts

In a medium saucepan, combine water, dry gelatin, and dry pudding mix. Mix well to combine. Stir in cherries. Cook over medium heat until mixture thickens and starts to boil. Remove from heat. Stir in almond extract. Cool for 5 minutes. Pour mixture into piecrust. Refrigerate for about 2 hours. In a medium bowl, stir cream cheese with a spoon until soft. Add Cool Whip Lite, vanilla extract, and sugar substitute. Spread mixture evenly over set pie filling. Sprinkle walnuts evenly over top. Refrigerate until ready to serve.

Each serving equals:

HE: ⅔ Pr, ½ Fr, ½ Br, ¼ Fa, ¾ Sl, 8 OC
201 Calories, 7 gm Fa, 7 gm Pr, 27 gm Ca, 372 mg So, 1 Fi
DIABETIC: 1 Fr, 1 St, 1 Fa

Cherries Jubilee Pie

This "uptown" dessert can be enjoyed in any town, anytime. Best of all, you won't run the risk of setting the kitchen on fire!

☻ Serves 8

> 1 (4-serving) package Jell-O sugar-free instant vanilla
>   pudding mix
> ⅔ cup Carnation nonfat dry milk powder
> 1¼ cups water
> 1 cup Cool Whip Lite ☆
> ½ teaspoon brandy extract
> 2 cups (12 ounces) pitted bing cherries
> 1 (6-ounce) Keebler butter-flavored piecrust

In a medium bowl, combine dry pudding mix and dry milk powder. Add water. Mix well using a wire whisk. Blend in ½ cup Cool Whip Lite and brandy extract. Fold in cherries. Pour mixture into piecrust. Refrigerate until set, about 15 minutes. Spread remaining ½ cup Cool Whip Lite evenly over top. Refrigerate until ready to serve.

Each serving equals:

HE: ½ Br, ½ Fr, ¼ SM, ¾ Sl, 19 OC

189 Calories, 6 gm Fa, 3 gm Pr, 31 gm Ca, 316 mg So, 1 Fi

DIABETIC: 1 St, 1 Fr, 1 Fa

Fresh Peach Pie

Is there a better summer fruit than a perfectly ripe peach? This is my daughter, Becky's, favorite fruit pie. She says it's like eating fresh peaches, only better! ☻ Serves 8

> 2 cups peaches, peeled and sliced (4 medium)
> 1 (6-ounce) Keebler butter-flavored or graham-cracker
>   piecrust
> 1 (4-serving) package Jell-O sugar-free lemon gelatin
> 1 (4-serving) package Jell-O sugar-free vanilla cook-and-
>   serve pudding mix
> 1½ cups water
> ½ cup Cool Whip Lite
> Dash nutmeg

Layer peaches in piecrust. In a medium saucepan, combine dry gelatin, dry pudding mix, and water. Cook over medium heat, stirring constantly, until mixture thickens and starts to boil. Pour hot mixture over peaches. Refrigerate until set, about 2 hours. When serving, top each piece with 1 tablespoon Cool Whip Lite and sprinkle with a dash of nutmeg.

Each serving equals:

HE: ½ Br, ½ Fr, ½ Sl, 32 OC

151 Calories, 5 gm Fa, 2 gm Pr, 24 gm Ca, 222 mg So, 1 Fi

DIABETIC: 1 St, 1 Fa, ½ Fr

Fruit-Cocktail Chiffon Pie

Take this pie to the next family potluck and watch it disappear almost as fast as you can cut it. It's really a pie from the '50s updated deliciously for the families of today. If you haven't eaten fruit cocktail since you were a kid, it'll make you feel like one again. ☻ Serves 8

> 1 (8-ounce) package Philadelphia fat-free cream cheese
> 1 (4-serving) package Jell-O sugar-free instant vanilla
>   pudding mix
> ⅔ cup Carnation nonfat dry milk powder
> 1 cup water
> 1 cup Cool Whip Lite ☆
> 2 cups (one 16-ounce can) canned fruit cocktail, packed in
>   its own juice, drained
> 1 (6-ounce) Keebler graham-cracker piecrust

In large mixing bowl stir cream cheese with spoon until soft. Add dry pudding mix, dry milk powder, and water. Mix well using a wire whisk. Fold in ½ cup Cool Whip Lite. Add fruit cocktail. Mix gently to combine. Pour mixture into piecrust. Refrigerate until ready to serve. When serving, top each piece with 1 tablespoon Cool Whip Lite.

Each serving equals:

HE: ½ Br, ½ Fr, ½ Pr, ¼ SM, ¾ Sl, 19 OC

221 Calories, 7 gm Fa, 8 gm Pr, 31 gm Ca, 439 mg So, 1 Fi

DIABETIC: 1 St, 1 Fr, 1 Fa

Rhubarb Fluff Pie

They don't call rhubarb the "pie plant" for nothing! This pie is so good, it'll put smiles on the faces of people who were pretty sure they didn't like rhubarb. If you've never cooked with it before, give this pie a try. ☻ Serves 8

4 cups chopped rhubarb
1 cup water
1 (4-serving) package Jell-O sugar-free strawberry gelatin
1 (4-serving) package Jell-O sugar-free vanilla cook-and-
serve pudding mix
1½ cups Cool Whip Lite
1 (6-ounce) Keebler graham-cracker piecrust

In a medium saucepan, combine chopped rhubarb, water, dry gelatin, and dry pudding mix. Bring mixture to a boil, stirring often. Lower heat and simmer until rhubarb is soft, about 10 minutes, stirring often. Remove from heat. Let cool until almost set; then whip until thick with electric mixer. Fold in Cool Whip Lite. Pour mixture into piecrust. Refrigerate for at least 2 hours before serving.

Each serving equals:

HE: 1 Ve, ½ Br, 1 Sl, 8 OC
171 Calories, 7 gm Fa, 2 gm Pr, 25 gm Ca, 250 mg So, 2 Fi
DIABETIC: 1½ St, 1 Fa

Blueberry-Banana Cream Pie

If you love bananas and blueberries (the best B-word fruits), then this beautiful, no-bake cream pie will deliver a *banquet*—yes, another B word—to your taste buds! ☻ Serves 8

1 cup sliced banana, (2 medium)
1½ cups fresh blueberries ☆
1 (6-ounce) Keebler butter-flavored piecrust
1 (4-serving) package Jell-O sugar-free instant banana
pudding mix
⅔ cup Carnation nonfat dry milk powder
1⅓ cups water
¾ cup Cool Whip Lite ☆

Place banana and 1¼ cups blueberries in piecrust. In a medium bowl, combine dry pudding mix and dry milk powder. Add water. Mix well using a wire whisk. Blend in ¼ cup Cool Whip Lite. Pour mixture evenly over fruit. Refrigerate for about 15 minutes. Spread remaining ½ cup Cool Whip Lite evenly over filling. Sprinkle remaining ¼ cup blueberries over top. Refrigerate until ready to serve.

Each serving equals:

HE: ½ Br, ½ Fr, ¼ SM, ¾ Sl, 15 OC

189 calories, 6 gm Fa, 3 gm Pr, 31 gm Ca, 323 mg So, 2 Fi

DIABETIC: 1 St, 1 Fr, 1 Fa

Becky's Southern
Banana-Butterscotch Cream Pie

This pie was born when my daughter, Becky, came home to visit one time. You know how the "Mommy thing" works. When the kids visit, we have to cook their most favorite foods—the ones they've loved since they were old enough to eat baby food, the ones we always make to celebrate special occasions. Becky is happy to share her namesake dessert and hopes you enjoy it as much as she does. ● Serves 8

> 2 cup sliced banana, (2 medium)
> 1 (6-ounce) Keebler graham-cracker piecrust
> 1 (4-serving) package Jell-O sugar-free instant butterscotch
>   pudding mix
> 2/3 cup Carnation nonfat dry milk powder
> 1 cup water
> 1/4 cup Cary's reduced-calorie maple syrup
> 3/4 cup Cool Whip Lite ☆
> 2 tablespoons (1/2 ounce) chopped pecans

Place sliced bananas in piecrust. In a medium bowl, combine dry pudding mix and dry milk powder. In 2-cup glass measuring cup, combine water and maple syrup. Add liquid mixture to dry pudding mixture. Mix well using a wire whisk. Blend in 1/4 cup Cool Whip Lite. Spread mixture evenly over bananas. Refrigerate for about 15 minutes. Spread remaining 1/2 cup Cool Whip Lite evenly over filling. Sprinkle pecans evenly over top. Refrigerate until ready to serve.

Each serving equals:

HE: 1/2 Br, 1/2 Fr, 1/4 SM, 1/4 Fa, 1 Sl
201 calories, 7 gm Fa, 3 gm Pr, 31 gm Ca, 356 mg So, 2 Fi
DIABETIC: 1 St, 1 Fr, 1 Fa

Simply Superb
Banana Cream Pie

When my printer, Tom, insisted this pie was too good to have just any old name, I decided to have a pie-naming contest. One of my newsletter readers came up with the winning name. You guessed right if you thought Tom was the judge.   ☻   Serves 8

> 2 cups sliced banana (2 medium)
> 1 (6-ounce) Keebler chocolate-flavored piecrust
> 1 (4-serving) package Jell-O sugar-free instant banana
>   pudding mix
> ⅔ cup Carnation nonfat dry milk powder
> 1⅓ cups water
> 1 cup Cool Whip Lite ☆
> 1 tablespoon chocolate syrup

Layer bananas on bottom of piecrust. In a medium bowl, combine dry pudding mix and dry milk powder. Add water. Mix well using a wire whisk. Blend in ¼ cup Cool Whip Lite. Pour mixture over bananas. Refrigerate for about 15 minutes. Spread remaining ¾ cup Cool Whip Lite evenly over filling. Drizzle chocolate syrup over top. Refrigerate until ready to serve.

Each serving equals:

HE: ½ Br, ½ Fr, ¼ SM, 1 Sl, 4 OC

200 Calories, 6 gm Fa, 4 gm Pr, 32 gm Ca, 298 mg So, 1 Fi

DIABETIC: 1 St, 1 Fa, 1 Fr

Butterscotch-Raisin Meringue Pie

If you always thought meringue pies were too much trouble *and* too loaded with fats and sugars, why don't you give this one a whirl? This recipe will easily disprove those beliefs—and provide a delicious taste treat with this unusual combination of flavors.

○ Serves 8

1 Pillsbury refrigerated unbaked
   9-inch piecrust
1 (4-serving) package Jell-O
   sugar-free vanilla cook-and-
   serve pudding mix
2 cups skim milk
1 (4-serving) package Jell-O
   sugar-free instant butterscotch
   pudding mix

½ cup raisins
6 egg whites
6 tablespoons Sprinkle Sweet or
   Sugar Twin
1 teaspoon vanilla extract

Bake piecrust according to package directions. Cool. In a medium saucepan, combine dry vanilla pudding mix and skim milk. Cook over medium heat, stirring constantly, until mixture comes to a boil. Remove from heat. Cool 10 minutes. Stir in dry instant butterscotch pudding mix and raisins. Pour mixture into cooled piecrust. In a medium bowl, whip egg whites with electric mixer until fluffy. Add Sprinkle Sweet and vanilla extract. Continue whipping until soft peaks form. Spread evenly over filling, being sure to seal completely to edges of piecrust. Bake at 425 degrees for 6 to 7 minutes or until meringue starts to brown. Cool on wire rack. Refrigerate leftovers.

Hints: 1. Eggs beat best at room temperature.
2. Meringue pie cuts easily if you dip your sharp knife in warm water before slicing.

Each serving equals:

HE: ½ Br, ½ Fr, ¼ SM, ¼ Pr, ¾ Sl, 17 OC
208 Calories, 7 gm Fa, 6 gm Pr, 30 gm Ca, 446 mg So, 2 Fi
DIABETIC: 1 Fr, 1 Fa, 1 St

Mary Rita's
Emergency Raisin Cream Pie

This pie was created one evening when a woman named Mary
Rita called me at 6:10 P.M. and had to be at a church potluck at
7:00 P.M. that night. She needed a quick raisin cream pie to take
with her. I made this up on the spot, tested it, called her back five
minutes later, and told her it was a go! I hope you enjoy it as
much as my testers and Mary Rita did. ● Serves 8

> 1 (4-serving) package Jell-O sugar-free instant vanilla
>   pudding mix
> ⅔ cup Carnation nonfat dry milk powder
> 1⅓ cups water
> 1 cup Cool Whip Lite ☆
> ½ teaspoon vanilla extract
> 1 cup raisins
> 1 (6-ounce) Keebler butter-flavored piecrust
> Dash nutmeg

In a large bowl, combine dry pudding mix and dry milk pow-
der. Add water. Mix well using a wire whisk. Blend in ¼ cup Cool
Whip Lite, vanilla extract, and raisins. Spread mixture into
piecrust. Let set about 15 minutes. Spread remaining ¾ cup Cool
Whip Lite evenly over filling. Sprinkle nutmeg lightly over top.
Refrigerate until ready to serve.

Hint: To plump up raisins without "cooking," place in glass measuring cup and microwave on HIGH for 45 seconds.

Each serving equals:
   HE: 1 Fr, ½ Br, ¼ SM, ¾ Sl, 19 OC
   220 Calories, 6 gm Fa, 3 gm Pr, 40 gm Ca, 318 mg So, 3 Fi
   DIABETIC: 1 Fr, 1 St, 1 Fa

Pumpkin Chiffon Pie

Our Pilgrim fathers (and mothers) would be proud of this "modern-day" pumpkin treat. Try this for a Halloween party, and you're certain to be begged for a repeat performance by Thanksgiving. ☺ Serves 8

> 2 cups (one 16-ounce can) canned pumpkin
> 1 (4-serving) package Jell-O sugar-free instant vanilla
>   pudding mix
> ⅔ cup Carnation nonfat dry milk powder
> 1 teaspoon pumpkin-pie spice
> ¾ cup water
> 1 cup Cool Whip Lite ☆
> 1 (6-ounce) Keebler graham-cracker piecrust
> 2 tablespoons (½ ounce) chopped pecans

In a medium bowl, combine canned pumpkin, dry pudding mix, dry milk powder, pumpkin-pie spice, and water. Mix well using a wire whisk. Blend in ¼ cup Cool Whip Lite. Pour mixture into piecrust. Refrigerate for about 15 minutes. Spread remaining ¾ cup Cool Whip Lite over top of set filling. Sprinkle pecans evenly on top. Refrigerate until ready to serve.

Each serving equals:

HE: ½ Br, ½ Ve, ¼ SM, ¼ Fa, ¾ Sl, 19 OC

206 Calories, 8 gm Fa, 4 gm Pr, 30 gm Ca, 350 mg So, 3 Fi

DIABETIC: 2 St, 1 Fa

Frost on the Pumpkin Patch Pie ❄

Pumpkin and coconut is another unusual taste combination. Don't turn your nose up until you try it. My taste testers said it was one of the most beautiful-looking and great-tasting pumpkin pies they had ever tried! And if you never thought of combining pumpkin with butterscotch pudding mix, after only one bite, you will be glad I did. ● Serves 8

1 (4-serving) package Jell-O sugar-free instant butterscotch
    pudding mix
2/3 cup Carnation nonfat dry milk powder
1 teaspoon pumpkin-pie spice
2 cups (one 16-ounce can) canned pumpkin
1 cup Cool Whip Lite ☆
1 (6-ounce) Keebler chocolate-flavored piecrust
1/2 teaspoon coconut extract
1 tablespoon (1/4 ounce) mini chocolate chips
2 tablespoons flaked coconut

In a large bowl, combine dry pudding mix, dry milk powder, and pumpkin-pie spice. Add pumpkin. Mix well, using a wire whisk. Blend in 1/4 cup Cool Whip Lite. Pour mixture into piecrust. Refrigerate for about 15 minutes. In a small bowl, combine remaining 3/4 cup Cool Whip Lite and coconut extract. Frost top of pie with mixture. Sprinkle mini chocolate chips and coconut evenly over top. Refrigerate until ready to serve.

Each serving equals:

HE: 1/2 Br, 1/2 Ve, 1/4 SM, 1 Sl, 7 OC
199 Calories, 7 gm Fa, 4 gm Pr, 30 gm Ca, 302 mg So, 3 Fi
DIABETIC: 2 St, 1 Fa

Paradise Pumpkin Pie

Here's another great combo: pumpkin and pineapple. When you add butterscotch to that pair, you get something very close to paradise—taste it and see if you agree. ●   Serves 8

> 1 (4-serving) package Jell-O sugar-free instant butterscotch
>   pudding mix
> ²/₃ cup Carnation nonfat dry milk powder
> 1 teaspoon pumpkin-pie seasoning
> 1 cup (one 8-ounce can) canned crushed pineapple, packed
>   in its own juice, drained (reserve liquid)
> 1 cup water
> 2 cups (one 16-ounce can) canned pumpkin
> 1 (6-ounce) Keebler graham-cracker piecrust
> ³/₄ cup Cool Whip Lite
> ½ teaspoon coconut extract
> 2 tablespoons flaked coconut
> 2 tablespoons (½ ounce) chopped pecans

In a large bowl, combine dry pudding mix, dry milk powder, and pumpkin-pie seasoning. Add water, reserved pineapple juice, and canned pumpkin. Mix well using a wire whisk. Pour mixture into graham-cracker crust. Refrigerate for about 15 minutes. In a small bowl, combine drained crushed pineapple, Cool Whip Lite, and coconut extract. Frost top of pie with pineapple mixture. Sprinkle flaked coconut and pecans evenly over top. Refrigerate until ready to serve.

Each serving equals:

HE: ½ Br, ½ Ve, ¼ SM, ¼ Fr, ¼ Fa, 1 Sl, 2 OC
222 Calories, 8 gm Fa, 4 gm Pr, 34 gm Ca, 352 mg So, 3 Fi
DIABETIC: 2 St, 1 Fa

Triple-Layer Party Pie

The more layers in a dessert, the more possibilities—don't you agree? My good friend Vince says you can have a party in your mouth with the flavors of this pie. ● Serves 8

> 1 (4-serving) package Jell-O sugar-free instant butterscotch pudding mix
> 1⅓ cups Carnation nonfat dry milk powder ☆
> 2½ cups water ☆
> 1 (6-ounce) Keebler chocolate-flavored piecrust
> 1 (4-serving) package Jell-O sugar-free instant chocolate pudding mix
> ½ cup Cool Whip Lite
> 2 tablespoons (½ ounce) chopped pecans
> 1 tablespoon (¼ ounce) mini chocolate chips

In a medium bowl, combine dry butterscotch pudding mix, ⅔ cup dry milk powder, and 1¼ cups water. Mix well, using a wire whisk. Pour mixture into piecrust. In a medium bowl, combine dry chocolate pudding mix, remaining ⅔ cup dry milk powder, and remaining 1¼ cups water. Mix well, using a wire whisk. Pour mixture over butterscotch layer. Refrigerate for about 15 minutes. Before serving, spread Cool Whip Lite evenly over chocolate layer. Sprinkle pecans and mini chocolate chips evenly over top. Refrigerate until ready to serve.

Each serving equals:

HE: ½ Br, ½ SM, ¼ Fa, 1 Sl, 8 OC

217 Calories, 7 gm Fa, 6 gm Pr, 32 gm Ca, 487 mg So, 1 Fi

DIABETIC: 2 St, 1 Fa, ½ SM

Chocolate–Peanut Butter Pie

This one was created while I was on my morning walk through DeWitt. I let my mind wander along with my feet, and I wound up with this chocolate winner. I know you'll agree that chocolate and peanut butter walk best "hand in hand." ○ Serves 8

> 3 tablespoons Peter Pan reduced-fat creamy peanut butter
> 1 (4-serving) package Jell-O sugar-free instant chocolate
>   pudding mix
> ⅔ cup Carnation nonfat dry milk powder
> 1½ cups water
> 1 (6-ounce) Keebler butter-flavored piecrust
> ½ cup Cool Whip Lite
> 2 tablespoons (½ ounce) chopped dry-roasted peanuts

Soften peanut butter to room temperature. In a medium bowl, combine dry pudding mix, dry milk powder, and water. Mix well, using a wire whisk. Blend in softened peanut butter. Pour mixture into piecrust. Refrigerate for about 15 minutes. Spread Cool Whip Lite evenly over set filling. Sprinkle chopped peanuts evenly over top. Refrigerate until ready to serve.

Each serving equals:

HE: ½ Fa, ½ Br, ⅓ Pr, ¼ SM, ¾ Sl, 14 OC

209 Calories, 10 gm Fa, 5 gm Pr, 25 gm Ca, 346 mg So, 1 Fi

DIABETIC: 1½ Fa, 1 St, ½ SM

Choco-Mint Pie

You can "bank" on all the compliments you'll receive when you serve this attractive mint pie to family and friends. My sister Regina says the recipe for this chocolate treasure should be kept in Fort Knox, it's so good! ☺ Serves 8

> 1 (4-serving) package Jell-O sugar-free instant vanilla
>   pudding mix
> ⅔ cup Carnation nonfat dry milk powder
> 1¼ cups water
> ½ teaspoon mint extract
> 2–3 drops green food coloring
> 1 cup Cool Whip Lite
> 2 tablespoons (½ ounce) mini chocolate chips
> 1 (6-ounce) Keebler chocolate-flavored piecrust

In a medium bowl, combine dry pudding mix, dry milk powder, and water. Mix well, using a wire whisk. Fold in mint extract, green food coloring, and Cool Whip Lite. Stir in chocolate chips. Pour mixture into piecrust. Refrigerate until ready to serve.

Each serving equals:

HE: ½ Br, ¼ SM, 1 Sl, 7 OC
169 Calories, 6 gm Fa, 3 gm Pr, 25 gm Ca, 291 mg So, 1 Fi
DIABETIC: 1½ St, 1 Fa

Almond Rejoice Pie

I always read my mail—I never know when something someone writes will trigger a great recipe idea. This pie was created when a woman sent me a note asking me to come up with a dessert that remotely resembled her favorite candy bar. ☉   Serves 8

> 1 (4-serving) package Jell-O sugar-free instant chocolate
>   pudding mix
> ⅔ cup Carnation nonfat dry milk powder
> 1⅓ cups water
> 1½ teaspoons coconut extract ☆
> 1 cup Cool Whip Lite ☆
> ¼ cup (1 ounce) chopped almonds
> 1 (6-ounce) Keebler chocolate-flavored piecrust
> 1 tablespoon (¼ ounce) miniature chocolate chips
> 2 tablespoons flaked coconut

In a medium bowl, combine dry pudding mix and dry milk powder. Add water. Mix well, using a wire whisk. Blend in ½ teaspoon coconut extract and ¼ cup Cool Whip Lite. Add almonds. Mix well. Pour mixture into piecrust. Refrigerate for about 15 minutes. In a small bowl, combine remaining ¾ cup Cool Whip Lite and remaining 1 teaspoon coconut extract. Spread mixture evenly over filling. Sprinkle mini chocolate chips and coconut evenly over top. Refrigerate until ready to serve.

Each serving equals:

HE: ½ Br, ¼ SM, ¼ Fa, 1 Sl, 14 OC
207 Calories, 9 gm Fa, 4 gm Pr, 27 gm Ca, 294 mg So, 1 Fi
DIABETIC: 2 St, 1 Fa

Blueberry Mountain Cheesecake ❄

I'm not kidding . . . if it takes you longer than three minutes from beginning to end to make this magnificent cheesecake, you're doing something in the kitchen besides cooking! ● Serves 8

> 2 (8-ounce) packages Philadelphia fat-free cream cheese
> 1 (4-serving) package Jell-O sugar-free instant vanilla pudding mix
> 2/3 cup Carnation nonfat dry milk powder
> 1 cup Diet Mountain Dew
> 3/4 cup Cool Whip Lite ☆
> 1 1/2 teaspoons coconut extract ☆
> 1 (6-ounce) Keebler butter-flavored piecrust
> 1/2 cup blueberry spreadable fruit spread
> 2 tablespoons flaked coconut

In a large bowl, stir cream cheese with a spoon until soft. Add dry pudding mix, dry milk powder, and Diet Mountain Dew. Mix well, using a wire whisk. Blend in 1/4 cup Cool Whip Lite and 1 teaspoon coconut extract. Pour mixture into piecrust. Refrigerate for about 15 minutes. In a small bowl, combine blueberry spreadable fruit, remaining 1/2 teaspoon coconut extract, and remaining 1/2 cup Cool Whip Lite. Spread blueberry mixture evenly over cheesecake filling. Sprinkle coconut evenly over top. Refrigerate until ready to serve.

Hint: Diet 7UP, Diet Slice, or even plain water can be used in place of the Diet Mountain Dew.

Each serving equals:

HE: 1 Fr, 1 Pr, 1/2 Br, 1/4 SM, 3/4 Sl, 19 OC

251 Calories, 6 gm Fa, 11 gm Pr, 38 gm Ca, 682 mg So, 1 Fi

DIABETIC: 1 1/2 St, 1 Fr, 1 Pr, 1/2 Fa

Piña Colada Cheesecake

This quick cheesecake has all the flavor of the islands without any of the guilt. Kick back and think "tropical breezes" when savoring this taste sensation. Isn't it amazing what a little coconut and pineapple can do for your stress level? ◐ Serves 8

> 2 (8-ounce) packages Philadelphia fat-free cream cheese
> 1 (4-serving) package Jell-O sugar-free instant vanilla
>   pudding mix
> ²/₃ cup Carnation nonfat dry milk powder
> 1 cup (one 8-ounce can) canned crushed pineapple, packed
>   in its own juice, undrained
> 1½ teaspoons coconut extract ☆
> 1 teaspoon rum extract
> 1 cup Cool Whip Lite ☆
> 1 (6-ounce) Keebler graham-cracker piecrust
> 2 tablespoons flaked coconut

In a medium bowl, stir cream cheese with a spoon until soft. Add dry pudding mix, dry milk powder, and pineapple with juice. Mix well, using a wire whisk. Blend in 1 teaspoon coconut extract, rum extract, and ¼ cup Cool Whip Lite. Spread mixture evenly into piecrust. Refrigerate for about 15 minutes. In a small bowl, combine remaining ¾ cup Cool Whip Lite and remaining ½ teaspoon coconut extract. Spread mixture evenly over cheesecake filling. Sprinkle coconut evenly over top. Refrigerate until ready to serve.

Each serving equals:

HE: 1 Pr, ½ Br, ¼ SM, ¼ Fr, 1 SI, 2 OC
233 Calories, 7 gm Fa, 11 gm Pr, 31 gm Ca, 684 mg So, 1 Fi
DIABETIC: 2 St, 1 Mt, ½ Fa

Chocolateville

Mocha Cheesecake

If you love chocolate in any form, I guarantee you will love this luscious dessert! (If you let on to others that it took only minutes to prepare, you're not taking advantage of the true impact of this cheesecake.) ● Serves 8

> 2 (8-ounce) packages Philadelphia fat-free cream cheese
> 1 (4-serving) package Jell-O sugar-free instant chocolate fudge pudding mix
> ⅔ cup Carnation nonfat dry milk powder
> 1 cup cold coffee
> 1 (6-ounce) Keebler chocolate-flavored piecrust
> ¾ cup Cool Whip Lite
> ½ teaspoon vanilla extract
> 2 teaspoons unsweetened cocoa
> Sugar substitute to equal 2 teaspoons sugar
> 1 tablespoon (¼ ounce) mini chocolate chips

In a medium bowl, stir cream cheese with a spoon until soft. Add dry pudding mix, dry milk powder, and coffee. Mix well, using a wire whisk. Spread mixture evenly into piecrust. Refrigerate for about 15 minutes. In a small bowl combine Cool Whip Lite, vanilla extract, cocoa, and sugar substitute. Spread mixture evenly over cheesecake filling. Sprinkle mini chocolate chips evenly over top. Refrigerate until ready to serve.

Each serving equals:

HE: 1 Pr, ½ Br, ¼ SM, 1 Sl, 3 OC

223 Calories, 7 gm Fa, 12 gm Pr, 28 gm Ca, 632 mg So, 1 Fi

DIABETIC: 2 St, 1 Mt, 1 Fa

Cabot Cove
Chocolate Cheesecake

My family and friends sometimes call me "Jessica" because I love to ride my bike all over DeWitt and sleuth out the excess fats and sugars in "common folk" recipes. So I think it's only fitting that I create a cheesecake named in honor of the town where the greatest woman detective of our time lives. ☻ Serves 8

2 (8-ounce) packages
Philadelphia fat-free cream
cheese
1 (4-serving) package Jell-O
sugar-free instant chocolate
fudge pudding mix
⅔ cup Carnation nonfat dry milk
powder
1 cup water
1½ teaspoons almond extract ☆

1 cup Cool Whip Lite ☆
1 (6-ounce) Keebler chocolate-
flavored piecrust
2 teaspoons Nestlé's Quik sugar-
free instant chocolate drink
mix
1 tablespoon (¼ ounce) chopped
almonds
1 tablespoon (¼ ounce) mini
chocolate chips

In a large bowl, stir cream cheese with a spoon until soft. Add dry pudding mix, dry milk powder, and water. Mix well, using a wire whisk. Stir in 1 teaspoon almond extract and ¼ cup Cool Whip Lite. Pour mixture into piecrust. Refrigerate for about 15 minutes. In a small bowl, combine remaining ¾ cup Cool Whip Lite, remaining ½ teaspoon almond extract, and instant chocolate drink mix. Spread mixture evenly over cheesecake filling. Sprinkle almonds and mini chocolate chips evenly over top. Refrigerate until ready to serve.

Each serving equals:

HE: 1 Pr, ½ Br, ¼ SM, 1 Sl, 17 OC

215 Calories, 7 gm Fa, 12 gm Pr, 26 gm Ca, 631 mg So, 1 Fi

DIABETIC: 2 St, 1 Fa

This and That

I created this section of the book for those recipes that just didn't
seem to fit anywhere else—dishes I hope will make you say, "I love
this" and "I want to taste that!" I've gathered some great breakfast
treats and healthy muffins, lively brunch dishes and spicy party dips, a
sandwich filling and my favorite punch, among others. I want to show
you that—no matter the occasion or time of day—Healthy Exchanges®
offers you so many wonderful opportunities to eat well and still enjoy
the best possible health.

Breakfast Pizza

Here's a great way to begin the morning. This easy "pizza" is as tasty to eat as it is simple to prepare (a good thing for those of you who aren't the best early risers!). If you love peanut butter as much as I do, this is a delicious way to ration the amount of peanut butter you eat—and still savor that creamy, nutty flavor.

● Serves 4

1 (4-ounce) can Pillsbury refrigerated crescent rolls
½ cup (4 ounces) Philadelphia fat-free cream cheese
½ teaspoon vanilla extract
1 tablespoon Peter Pan reduced-fat chunky peanut butter
1 cup sliced banana (1 medium)

Preheat oven to 375 degrees. Spray a 9-inch pie plate with butter-flavored cooking spray. Press in crescent rolls, being sure to seal perforations. Bake 10 minutes. Cool on wire rack. In a small bowl, stir cream cheese with a spoon until soft. Stir in vanilla extract and peanut butter. Spread mixture evenly over cooled crust. Sprinkle sliced banana over top. Serve at once.

Each serving equals:

HE: 1 Pr, 1 Br, ½ Fa, ½ Fr
205 Calories, 9 gm Fa, 8 gm Pr, 23 gm Ca, 439 mg So, 2 Fi
DIABETIC: 1 Mt, 1 St, 1 Fa, ½ Fr

Baked Potato-Egg Nests

How about preparing these for the family on a weekend morning when you may have a few more minutes to cook and visit around the breakfast table? I think everyone will be pleased with both the tummy-warming "nests" *and* the conversation. ☻ Serves 4

2 teaspoons reduced-calorie margarine

1/4 cup chopped onion

1/4 cup chopped green bell pepper

4 cups (15 ounces) frozen shredded potatoes, slightly thawed, or raw shredded potatoes

3/4 cup (3 ounces) Kraft shredded reduced-fat Cheddar cheese ☆

1/2 teaspoon salt

1/8 teaspoon lemon pepper

4 eggs or equivalent in egg substitute

Preheat oven to 325 degrees. In a large skillet, melt margarine. Add onion and green pepper. Sauté vegetables until tender-crisp. Stir in potatoes. Cook until potatoes are slightly browned, stirring occasionally. Remove from heat and cool slightly. Stir in 1/2 cup Cheddar cheese, salt, and lemon pepper. Spoon mixture evenly into 4 individual casseroles sprayed with butter-flavored cooking spray. Make an indentation in center of each mixture. Carefully break 1 egg or pour 1/4 of egg substitute into each indentation. Bake 10 to 20 minutes, depending on desired doneness. Top each with 1 tablespoon Cheddar cheese and bake another 2 to 3 minutes.

Each serving equals:

HE: 2 Pr (1 limited), 3/4 Br, 1/4 Ve, 1/4 Fa

221 Calories, 9 gm Fa, 15 gm Pr, 20 gm Ca, 570 mg So, 2 Fi

DIABETIC: 2 Mt, 1½ St, ½ Fa

Jiffy Eggs Benedict

This recipe retains the taste of the original, but I've speeded up the cooking process—and eliminated a lot of fat. I don't think anyone will notice that you took a short cut or two when they taste this elegant breakfast dish that makes any meal a real occasion. ❂ Serves 4

1 (10¾-ounce) can Campbell's Healthy Request Cream of
    Mushroom Soup
1 tablespoon dried parsley flakes
4 (1½-ounce) slices Dubuque 97% fat-free or other extra-
    lean ham
2 English muffins, split, toasted, and lightly sprayed with
    butter-flavored cooking spray
4 eggs, poached

In a medium saucepan, combine mushroom soup and parsley flakes. Simmer over low heat while browning ham. In a large skillet sprayed with butter-flavored cooking spray, lightly brown ham slices. For each serving, place slice of ham on muffin half. Cover ham with poached egg. Spoon soup mixture evenly over egg. Serve at once.

Hints: 1. A 1½-ounce slice of ham is usually about ¼ inch thick.
2. Egg substitute "fried" in nonstick skillet sprayed with butter-flavored cooking spray can be used in place of poached eggs.

Each serving equals:

HE: 1¾ Pr (1 limited), 1 Br, ½ Sl, 1 OC
220 Calories, 8 gm Fa, 16 gm Pr, 21 gm Ca, 872 mg So, 1 Fi
DIABETIC: 2 Mt, 1½ St

Rodeo Omelet Bake

Serve this up to all your cowboy or cowgirl "wannabees" and see if they don't "round up" the energy to start their busy days with a smile! "Home on the Range" was never this good. ☻ Serves 4

2 teaspoons reduced-calorie margarine

½ cup (3 ounces) diced Dubuque 97% fat-free or other extra-lean ham

¼ cup chopped green bell pepper

¼ cup chopped onion

6 eggs, slightly beaten, or equivalent in egg substitute

1 (10¾-ounce) can Campbell's Healthy Request Cream of Mushroom Soup

½ cup chunky salsa

Preheat oven to 350 degrees. Melt margarine in a large skillet. Add ham, green pepper, and onion; sauté until crisp-tender. Remove from heat. In a medium bowl, combine eggs and mushroom soup. Stir in slightly cooled ham mixture. Pour into an 8-by-8-inch baking dish sprayed with butter-flavored cooking spray. Place dish inside a larger pan that has 1 inch of water in it. Bake 30 minutes or until done in center. When serving, pour 2 tablespoons salsa sauce over each portion.

Each serving equals:

HE: 2 Pr (1½ limited), ½ Ve, ¼ Fa, ½ Sl, 1 OC

187 Calories, 10 gm Fa, 14 gm Pr, 10 gm Ca, 716 mg So, 1 Fi

DIABETIC: 2 Mt, 2 Ve, ½ Fa

Western Scramble

Here's my take on scrambled eggs with a western slant. Combining ham, veggies, and cheese makes your boring morning eggs something worth opening your eyes—and your mouth—for!

● Serves 4

4 eggs, slightly beaten, or equivalent in egg substitute
2 tablespoons skim milk
½ cup (one 2.5-ounce can) canned sliced mushrooms, drained
½ teaspoon lemon pepper
2 teaspoons reduced-calorie margarine
½ cup (3 ounces) diced Dubuque 97% fat-free or other extra-lean ham
¼ cup chopped green bell pepper
¼ cup chopped onion
¾ cup (3 ounces) Kraft shredded reduced-fat Cheddar cheese

In a medium bowl, combine eggs, skim milk, mushrooms, and lemon pepper. In a large skillet melt margarine. Add ham, green pepper, and onions. Sauté until vegetables are tender. Add egg mixture. Cook over low heat until eggs are almost set. Sprinkle top with Cheddar cheese. Cover for 2 to 3 minutes to allow cheese to melt.

Hint: Fresh mushrooms, when available, are a wonderful change of pace from canned. Simply sauté with ham and other vegetables.

Each serving equals:

HE: 2½ Pr (1 limited), ½ Ve, ¼ Fa, 4 OC
163 Calories, 9 gm Fa, 16 gm Pr, 4 gm Ca, 503 mg So, 1 Fi
DIABETIC: 2 Mt, 1 Free Ve, ½ Fa

Egg and Frankfurter Sandwich Filling

I know this combination sounds kind of silly, but you'll be happily surprised to discover it makes a very tasty sandwich. Kids of all ages go for this in a big way. ☻ Serves 4 (½ cup)

2 (1.6-ounce) Healthy Choice 97% fat-free frankfurters
2 hard-boiled eggs, cooled
1 cup chopped celery
¼ cup Kraft fat-free mayonnaise
½ teaspoon dried parsley flakes
⅛ teaspoon black pepper

Cook and cool frankfurters. Chop eggs and frankfurters into fine pieces and combine in a medium bowl. Add celery, mayonnaise, parsley flakes, and black pepper. Mix well to combine. Refrigerate for 2 hours.

Each serving equals:

HE: 1 Pr, ½ Ve, 12 OC
74 Calories, 3 gm Fa, 6 gm Pr, 6 gm Ca, 398 mg So, 1 Fi
DIABETIC: 1 Mt

Festive Noodles

with Poppy Seeds

If you've never tried poppy seeds, I think you'll be pleasantly surprised by how much flavor they add to this easy dish. Serve this festive side dish with meat loaf, ham slices, or grilled chicken breasts. It holds its own with just about any main dish you can possibly think to pair it up with. ● Serves 4 (½ cup)

½ cup frozen peas
1½ cups hot cooked noodles
1 tablespoon + 1 teaspoon reduced-calorie margarine
1 teaspoon poppy seeds
⅛ teaspoon black pepper

In a medium saucepan, combine peas and noodles. Add margarine, poppy seeds, and black pepper. Toss gently to combine. Cook over medium heat until heated through, stirring often.

Hint: 1¼ cups uncooked noodles usually make about 1½ cups cooked.

Each serving equals:

HE: 1 Br, ½ Fa, 4 OC
104 Calories, 2 gm Fa, 4 gm Pr, 17 gm Ca, 41 mg So, 2 Fi
DIABETIC: 1 St, ½ Fa

Applesauce-Oatmeal Muffins

Try mixing up a batch of these filling muffins and freezing the leftovers. They warm up wonderfully in the microwave when every minute counts during those morning rush hours.

● Serves 12

1 ½ cups (4 ½ ounces) uncooked oats
¾ cup flour
½ teaspoon cinnamon
1 teaspoon baking powder
½ teaspoon baking soda
¼ teaspoon salt
1 cup unsweetened applesauce
¼ cup skim milk
2 tablespoons + 2 teaspoons vegetable oil
3 tablespoons Brown Sugar Twin
1 egg, beaten, or equivalent in egg substitute
¼ cup raisins

Preheat oven to 350 degrees. In a large bowl, combine oats, flour, cinnamon, baking powder, baking soda, and salt. Add applesauce, milk, vegetable oil, Brown Sugar Twin, egg, and raisins. Spray muffin tins with butter-flavored cooking spray or line with paper liners. Fill 12 muffin wells ¾ full. Bake 20 to 25 minutes or until muffins test done.

Hint: Fill unused muffin wells with water. It protects the muffin tin and ensures even baking.

Each serving equals:

HE: 1 Br, ⅔ Fa, ⅓ Fr, 9 OC
118 Calories, 3 gm Fa, 3 gm Pr, 19 gm Ca, 114 mg So, 1 Fi
DIABETIC: 1 St, ½ Fr

Blueberry Yogurt Muffins

The blueberries shine in this easy muffin recipe. Fresh berries work best when you can get them, but frozen will do the trick out of season. ☻ Serves 8

1½ cups flour

1 tablespoon Sprinkle Sweet or Sugar Twin

2 tablespoons Brown Sugar Twin

1 teaspoon baking powder

½ teaspoon baking soda

¾ cup plain fat-free yogurt

1 egg, slightly beaten, or equivalent in egg substitute

2 tablespoons + 2 teaspoons vegetable oil

1½ cups fresh or frozen blueberries, thawed and drained

Preheat oven to 425 degrees. In a large bowl, combine flour, Sprinkle Sweet, Brown Sugar Twin, baking powder, and baking soda. Add yogurt, egg, and vegetable oil. Mix gently just to combine. Fold in blueberries. Spray muffin tins with butter-flavored cooking spray or line with paper liners. Fill 8 muffin wells ¾ full. Bake 20 to 25 minutes or until muffins test done.

Hint: Fill unusued muffin wells with water. It protects the muffin tin and ensures even baking.

Each serving equals:

HE: 1 Br, 1 Fa, ¼ Fr, ¼ Sl, 1 OC

155 Calories, 4 gm Fa, 5 gm Pr, 24 gm Ca, 117 mg So, 2 Fi

DIABETIC: 1 St, 1 Fa, ½ Fr

Salsa Dip

If you always thought fat-free products lacked flavor when the fat was removed, scoop up a taste of this creamy, spicy dip. After just one mouthful, I know you'll change your mind about fat-free foods prepared "my way." This dip is good for fresh veggies or crackers. ◦ Serves 8 (¼ cup)

> 1 (8-ounce) package Philadelphia fat-free cream cheese
> ¼ cup Kraft fat-free mayonnaise
> 1 cup chunky salsa

In a medium bowl, stir cream cheese with spoon until soft. Add mayonnaise. Mix well until light and fluffy. Blend in salsa. Refrigerate for at least 2 hours.

Each serving equals:

HE: ½ Pr, ¼ Ve, 4 OC

34 Calories, 0 gm Fa, 4 gm Pr, 4 gm Ca, 349 mg So, 0 Fi

DIABETIC: 1 Ve

Macho Man Dip

I shared samples of this dip at a bookstore autograph session. Two fifteen-year-old boys helped me name it. They said, "Real Men may not eat yogurt, but they sure would eat this dip." In addition to being a great dip, this is wonderful on a baked potato.

⊙   Serves 8 (¼ cup)

¾ cup plain fat-free yogurt
⅓ cup Carnation nonfat dry milk powder
1 cup chunky salsa
1 teaspoon dried parsley flakes

In a medium bowl, combine yogurt and dry milk powder. Add salsa and parsley flakes. Mix gently to combine. Cover and refrigerate until ready to serve.

Each serving equals:

HE: ¼ SM, ¼ Ve

28 Calories, 0 gm Fa, 2 gm Pr, 4 gm Ca, 150 mg So, 0 Fi

DIABETIC: 1 Ve

Vegetable Dip

One taste of this dip, and it's bound to become your favorite. The vegetable flakes are the "secret ingredient." It's the ideal dip to serve with raw vegetables.　❍　Serves 8 (¼ cup)

1 (8-ounce) package Philadelphia fat-free cream cheese
¾ cup Kraft fat-free mayonnaise
½ cup Kraft fat-free Western Dressing
2 tablespoons dried vegetable flakes
1 tablespoon dried onion flakes

In a medium bowl, stir cream cheese with a spoon until softened. Add mayonnaise, Western Dressing, vegetable flakes, and onion flakes. Mix gently to combine. Cover and refrigerate.

Each serving equals:
HE: ½ Pr, ¼ Sl, 13 OC
46 Calories, 0 gm Fa, 4 gm Pr, 5 gm Ca, 290 mg So, 0 Fi
DIABETIC: ½ St, ½ Mt

White House Punch

This party drink is more than delicious enough to be served in the nation's First House! It's as refreshing as it is attractive. What more could you ask of an easy thirst quencher?

○ Serves 6 (1 cup)

4 cups Ocean Spray reduced-calorie cranberry juice cocktail
2 cups Diet 7UP

In a large pitcher, combine cranberry juice cocktail and Diet 7UP. Mix well. Serve over ice. The recipe can be doubled and served in a punch bowl. Pour over 2 cups of ice cubes.

Hint: To make this beautiful to the eye, garnish with slices of fresh fruit.

Each serving equals:

HE: ⅔ Fr

36 Calories, 0 gm Fa, 0 gm Pr, 9 gm Ca, 16 mg So, 0 Fi

DIABETIC: ½ Fr

"Grandma's" Lemonade

This is so-o-o good that everyone who tries it is bound to ask, "You mean you went to *all* the trouble of making fresh lemonade for *me?*" I want you to flick a few drops of water on your forehead and say, "Yes, I did. And as long as you are good to me, I'll be happy to work that hard for you!" Let's keep it our secret that the actual preparation time is under 60 seconds.

○ Serves 8 (1 cup)

1 tub Crystal Light sugar-free lemonade mix
8 cups water
¼ of a lemon, unpeeled and unseeded

Prepare sugar-free lemonade according to package directions. Slice ¼ to ⅓ of a lemon, *including skin and seeds,* into chunks. Pour 2 cups of prepared lemonade into a blender; add lemon chunks and blend on HIGH for 30 to 45 seconds. Pour into the pitcher of lemonade mixture and mix well. Serve over ice and enjoy!

Hint: You can also use ¼ to ⅓ of an orange for Lemon-Orange Ade, or ⅛ to ¼ of a lime for Lemon-Lime Ade.

Each serving equals:

HE: 1 OC

1 Calorie, 0 gm Fa, 0 gm Pr, 0 gm Ca, less than 1 mg So, 0 Fi

DIABETIC: Free Food

Strawberry Daiquiri

All right, I confess. After I created this strawberry sensation, I *forced* myself to taste-test it *three* days in a row! No need to bother crushing ice—the frozen strawberries take care of that for you. P.S.: You don't need a designated driver after enjoying this refreshing nonalcoholic drink. ❂   Serves 4 (1 cup)

> 2 cups frozen strawberries, no sugar added
> 2 cups Diet Mountain Dew
> 2 tablespoons lemon juice
> 2 tablespoons lime juice
> 1 (4-serving) package Jell-O sugar-free strawberry gelatin

In a blender container, combine strawberries, Diet Mountain Dew, lemon juice, lime juice, and dry gelatin. Process on HIGH 15 seconds. Continue processing on HIGH until mixture is smooth. Pour into glasses.

Each serving equals:

HE: ½ Fr, 8 OC

35 Calories, 0 gm Fa, 2 gm Pr, 7 gm Ca, 75 mg So, 2 Fi

DIABETIC: ½ Fr

Index

Soups

Salads

Vegetables

Main Dishes

Desserts

THIS and THAT

Now That You've Seen the *Healthy Exchanges*® *Cookbook, Why Not Order the Healthy Exchanges*® *Food Newsletter?*

If you enjoyed the recipes in this cookbook and would like to cook up even more of these "common folk" healthy dishes, you may want to subscribe to the *Healthy Exchanges*® *Food Newsletter.*

This monthly twelve-page newsletter contains thirty-plus new recipes *every month* in such columns as:

•Reader's Exchange	•Snack Attack	•Main Dishes
•Dinner for Two	•Recipe Makeover	•Micro Corner
•Brown Bagging It	•Meatless Main Dishes	•Rise & Shine
•Special Requests	•Side Dishes	•Desserts
•Crock Pot Luck	•Our Small World	•Complete Meal

In addition to all the recipes, other regular features include:

•The Editor's Motivational Corner
•Dining Out Question & Answer
•Cooking Question & Answer
•New Product Alert
•Success Profiles of Winners in the Losing Game
•Everyday Athlete Exercise Tips

Just as in this cookbook, all *Healthy Exchanges*® *Food Newsletter* recipes are calculated in three distinct ways: (1) Weight-Loss Choices™, (2) Calories with Grams, and (3) Diabetic Exchanges.

The cost for a one-year (12-issue) subscription with a special Healthy Exchanges® three-ring binder to store the newsletters in is $26.50. To order, simply complete this form and mail to us *or* call our toll-free number and pay with your VISA or MasterCard.

_____ Yes, I want to subscribe to *The Healthy Exchanges Food Newsletter*
$26.50 Yearly Subscription Cost .... $ _____

_____ Foreign orders please add $6.00 for money exchange and extra
postage... $ _____

_____ I'm not sure, so please send me a sample copy at $2.50 .... $ _____

Total .... $ _____

Please make check payable to HEALTHY EXCHANGES or pay by
VISA/MasterCard

CARD NUMBER: _____ EXPIRATION DATE: _____
SIGNATURE: _____

Signature required for all credit card orders.

Or Order Toll-Free, using your credit card, at 1-800-766-8961

NAME: _____
ADDRESS: _____
CITY _____ STATE _____ ZIP _____
TELEPHONE: ( ) _____

*If additional orders for the newsletter are to be sent to an address other than the
one listed above, please use a separate sheet and attach to this form.*

MAIL TO: HEALTHY EXCHANGES
P.O. BOX 124
DeWitt, IA 52742-0124

1-800-766-8961 For Customer Orders
1-319-659-8234 For Customer Service

Thank you for your order, and for choosing to become a part of the Healthy
Exchanges family!